Woman as Spectator and Spectacle

Essays on Women and Media

Edited by

K. Durga Bhavani

C. Vijayasree

FOUNDATION®
BOOKS

Bangalore • Chennai • Delhi • Hyderabad • Kolkata • Mumbai • Pune

Published by
Cambridge University Press India Pvt. Ltd. under the imprint of
Foundation Books
CAMBRIDGE HOUSE
4381/4, Ansari Road, Daryaganj
New Delhi – 110002

C-22, C-Block, Brigade M.M., K.R. Road, Jayanagar, **Bangalore** 560 070
Plot No. 80, Service Industries, Shirvane, Sector-1, Nerul, **Navi Mumbai** 400 706
10 Raja Subodh Mullick Square, 2nd Floor, **Kolkata** 700013
21/1 (New No. 49), 1st Floor, Model School Road, Thousand Lights, **Chennai** 600 006
House No. 3-5-874/6/4, (Near Apollo Hospital), Hyderguda, **Hyderabad** 500 029
Agarwal Pride, 'A' Wing, 1308 Kasba Peth, Near Surya Hospital, **Pune** 411 011

First published 2010

ISBN 978-81-7596-768-7 (Paperback)

Typeset by Techastra Solutions Pvt. Ltd., Hyderabad

Cover design by Rahul Ganguly

Published by Manas Saikia for Cambridge University Press India Pvt. Ltd.
and Printed at Sanat Printers, Kundli.

Contents

Part II: Framing Women

Notes on Contributors

Urvashi Butalia (preface) is the co-founder of Kali for Women, India's first feminist publishing house. She is currently Director of Zubaan, an imprint of Kali. Her many publications include *Women and the Hindu Right: A Collection of Essays* (co-edited), *Speaking Peace: Women's Voices from Kashmir* (edited) and the award winning history of Partition, *The Other Side of Silence: Voices from the Partition of India*.

Ammu Joseph is an independent journalist. She is currently teaching at the Convergence Institute of Media, Management and Information Technology, Bangalore. She has contributed chapters to a number of books, including the recent *Encyclopedia of International Media and Communications* (Academic Press, USA, 2003), *Women and Media: International Perspectives* (edited by Karen Ross and Carolyn M. Byerly, Blackwell, UK, 2004), *Gender and Newsroom Cultures: Identities at Work* (edited by Marjan de Bruin and Karen Ross, Hampton Press, USA, 2004), and *Practising Journalism, Vol. II* (edited by Nalini Rajan, Sage, forthcoming). She was awarded the Donna Allen Award for Feminist Advocacy in 2003.

R. Amritavalli was a Professor in the Department of Media and Communication in the English and Foreign Languages University until recently. Currently, she is a Professor in the Department of Linguistics in the same university.

Bala Kothandaraman is (former) Professor and Head, Department of English, Osmania University. Along with Prof. Bernth Lindfors, she has co-edited three volumes of specially invited essays of *South Asian Responses* to each of Achebe, Ngugi, and Soyinka. She has published extensively on postcoloniality, theory, popular culture, and pedagogic concerns.

Kalpana Wandrekar is Reader in English at the University of Pune. Her areas of interest are diaspora, cross-cultural studies, comparative literature, gender studies, translations and Indian writing in English. Her published works include *The Ailing Aliens*.

K. Durga Bhavani is Professor of English at Osmania University, Hyderabad. She has specialized in English Language Teaching and Learning. She is involved in syllabus designing, teaching and producing material for various ESL and ESP courses in the University and the corporate sector. She has four books to her credit in the field of ELT and Stylistics and interpretation of Literature. She has also designed and taught a post graduate course in women and media in OU College for Women and worked on 'Translation in media' for the British Council interface project.

C. Mrunalini is a Professor and the Director in Centre for Comparative Studies at P. S. Telugu University. She was associated with World space Satellite Radio as a Consultant. She has over nine titles to her credit, which include short stories, criticism and translation. She has been associated with the media for the past 25 years.

Waheeda Sultana is a Reader, in the Department of Mass Communication and Journalism, Mangalore University, Karnataka, India. She has published several research articles on current media related issues in refereed journals.

Somdatta Mandal is Associate Professor and Head of the Department of English and Other Modern European Languages, Visva-Bharati, Santiniketan. Recipient of prestigious national and international awards like the Sahitya Akademi Prize for translation, the Fulbright, the Charles Wallace and the Rockefeller, she has published several articles and books. Her areas of interest are contemporary fiction, Film and Culture Studies, Diaspora studies and translation.

C. Vijayasree is Professor of English at Osmania University and is presently Director, Osmania University Centre for International Programmes. She has authored eleven books and has published over fifty research articles in national and international journals. She is well known for her work in the area of Postcolonial Literatures. Her many publications include *Mulk Raj Anand: The Raj and the Writer* (1998), *Suniti Namjoshi: An Artful Transgressor* (2001) and edited volumes of critical essays: *Writing the West* (2004) and *Nation and Imagination* (2007).

Shree Deepa is currently teaching in the University of Hyderabad. She is also an external faculty member in Osmania University, TEFLU and IIPM.

K. Lavanya is Assistant Professor in the Department of English, Hyderabad Central University.

Soumya Garima Jaipuriar teaches English Literature at St. Stephen's College, University of Delhi.

Preface

The debate on women and media has, over the years, become increasingly complex. Early issues of the positive or negative portrayal of women in the media have given way to questions of representation, of numbers, of the nuances of class, caste, region, religion, geography, to name only a few. With the exponential growth in all forms of media, whether print, broadcast, electronic, or those related to the Internet, to messaging and mobile telephony and so on, issues of access, of voice, of censorship and regulation, and indeed of reach have also become significant. Women are now much more visible in television programming, and in content. They are significant among the numbers of viewers and readers. They make up an important segment of the consumer market and are therefore the ones who are primarily addressed in advertising. And, increasingly, they are beginning to count among the numbers of media owners, gatekeepers and content creators.

These changes have also meant that questions relating to women and media have become more complex and troubled. Despite some seeming and some very real changes in the media, women still remain in the background in a number of ways. Media summits – increasingly popular today – mostly feature male media magnates and editors, with the occasional woman thrown in. And yet, no such event, whether it is a panel discussion, or a media summit, can actually take place without the anchors and organizers at least trying to include women – for if not in actuality, but at least in awareness there has been the realization that women are significant actors and they must find a place and a voice in the media.

Similarly, subjects that were earlier seen in somewhat stark or black and white terms, are no longer perceived to be thus. For example, debates on censorship now question who has the right to censor and whether or not there needs to be a regulatory authority at all. No longer is it only the State that can appoint itself the legitimate censor (and here too questions are being raised about whether or not States can give themselves this right) but censorship has also become something that is arbitrarily taken up by groups of individuals who see themselves as the moral guardians of society. Their very arbitrary nature and their claim that this or that media content should be removed because it hurts the sentiments of this or that community, forces the issue of whether or not there should be any kind of regulation. Pitted against this is women's claim that their sentiments are being hurt all the time, but this never gets any consideration. An equally important issue is that there is a legitimate concern among parents about the levels of violence and explicit sex in the media and children's exposure to these. Alongside this is the even more troubled and troublesome question of the expression of women's sexuality. This came up in particular some years ago when the by-now famous Hindi film song, "Choli ke Peeche", raised a furious debate among women's groups on issues of censorship and free expression.

Clearly, the number of issues are many, and discussion on these are not only important but necessary. With the supposed 'freeing' of the (electronic and broadcast) media from government controls, and with the entry of private, and often global, players, a whole host of new issues has come up. Public service broadcasting is now a thing of the past, with even channels like Doordarshan offering programme content that features mainly upper class, upper caste, and usually Hindu characters. Reading the newspapers or news magazines today, or indeed watching television or films, one can be forgiven for thinking that poverty does not exist in India anymore – at least that is what the media would have us believe. The poor are not sexy so they do not find a place in the media.

It is for this reason that books such as this one are important. They remind us that all is not well in the world of media, that simply because things have changed and many within the media have perfected the art of creating deceptive and illusory worlds, does not imply that everything has miraculously become all right. More than ever today, questions are being raised by women, and some men, within the world of media, and also by consumers of media. Further, the essays included here, by eminent academics and activists, also turn the lens on the alternatives that have come up. Have activist strategies to counter the hegemony of mainstream media been adequate? Or do they leave something to be desired? Indeed the essays here address a wide range of issues – from films, not only in Hindi but also in Telugu, to the roles women play in media, from soaps and what they do and how they do it, to directors and producers of the popular serials, to issues of cyberspace and access – all of these find consideration here.

Together they remind us of the importance of continuing the debate on women, and, women in, the media, and ensuring that resistance and change remain important at all times. The essays here also draw our attention to new ways of thinking about the issue of media, and the multiple roles the media plays in our lives.

URVASHI BUTALIA

Publisher and Writer

Introduction

If there is one single revolution which has decisively impacted the lives of the largest number of people in the twentieth century, it is the explosion in the field of media, and its reach. There is not a single social group which is outside the influence of media; not a single issue that is not mediated by media. In fact media has erased several borders and facilitated trafficking of images across barriers. Media constructs and deconstructs identities, prescribes and proscribes values, makes and unmakes lifestyles, creates and destroys icons, and simply mediates every aspect of our life. Even remote geographic areas are influenced by advertising, newspapers, magazines, radio, television, music, films and other print and electronic media. The mediated images and messages construct the very fabric of everyday life, knowledge and frameworks of reality. Given this omnipotence and omnipresence of media, it is imperative that we examine the ramifications of this huge apparatus for all sections of people.

In the last two decades Media Studies has quite rightly and understandably become a popular discipline operating under the broad rubric of Cultural Studies and has provided the necessary critical analyses of the developments in media from a variety of perspectives. One of the major concerns of media critics has been "the gendered structures and relationships between human beings on the inside of media industries who control the resources, determine the images, words, and sounds that we consume" (Ross and Byerly: 1). Equally important, of course, are the ways in which media technology, messages, and the agencies involved in production, distribution and consumption of media texts influence popular perceptions of gender. Exposing these issues is the aim of this anthology.

The broader academic study of media from a feminist perspective has bourgeoned over the last three decades beginning with Laura Mulvey's oft quoted essay, "Visual Pleasure and Narrative Cinema". The focus of much of the scholarship in the field has been on the ways in which gender, race and sexual identity enter into the construction and consumption of media messages. Questions about the implications of these media messages for the identities of the marginalized have been critically addressed. These aspects of media research actually emerged through various social movements – feminist, gay and lesbian, racial justice, postcolonial and dalit – in 1970's. Two aspects of media are negotiated in these studies – first is the role of media in reinforcing unequal status quo relationships and second is the capability of media to generate new ideas and usher change and liberation from the grids of hierarchy.

The women's readings of media have indeed come a long way from Mulvey's work which focuses on "representations of women in the media" to structuralist and post structuralist readings which insist on "analyzing gender as a mechanism that structures material and symbolic worlds and our experiences of them" (Van Zoonen: 33). The general developments in feminism such as Critical feminism, Cultural feminism and Postcolonial feminism – have had their impact on feminist media studies too. All these approaches attempt radical enquiries into gender and other relations of power in society and examine the ways in which media reinforces hierarchy in social structures. Critical feminist scholars of media draw on Marxist concepts such as "Critique of Capitalism" and examine how male-owned media industry exploits women's bodies and talent to consolidate their own profit and social power. Cultural feminist critics deploy Gramsci's concept of 'hegemony' to examine the subtle ways in which media manufactures consent for male dominance. The work of feminist postcolonial scholars has been to locate women in their historical contexts and examine the role of media in manipulating these contexts. They also show how colonial domination has not ceased with the termination of political control of the colonizing nations, but simply changed its countenance in the era of globalization which releases a flow of images through magazines, television, films, advertisements, fashion and other media forms from the powerful Euro-American nations into the rest of the world.

One more welcome development in media studies is the increasing attention paid by researchers to audience responses. In other words, inclusion of the feedback from the female audiences into feminist research on media has in fact democratized the space of feminist media studies considerably. Yet another locational aspect which becomes important is the production of media criticism from within – each linguistic and regional segment producing its own critical readings of the media discourses in its specific domain. It is important to stress the importance of the production of 'local' readings of media texts without however disparaging the importance of global media studies' readings or theories. While benefiting from the archive of critical knowledge on media produced internationally, it is important to produce 'local' knowledges focusing on specific developments in a particular linguistic and regional milieu. If the nuances of region, language and local cultures are not accounted for, the discipline of Cultural Studies will lose its primary purpose.

The present volume inhabits the analytical terrain charted by the various complex critical discourses developed by feminist critics of media, elaborated above. These developments are by no means complete but are still evolving, responding quickly and sensitively to the rapid changes occurring in the world mediated by global media. This volume is an attempt to bring together critical readings of several important developments in the Indian media in the last quarter of the twentieth century with a focus on the interconnections between media and women's issues. The subjects discussed range from questions of representation to the need for evolving a gender policy for the media. The focus is not only on women as objects in media representation but on women as producers as well as consumers of media texts. The diverse ways in which media and women's issues are intermeshed constitute the main thrust of this volume. The writers include media watchers, academics, researchers in media and actual performers in the media. Their studies emerge from their engagement with media in its local specificities be it Hindi films, advertisements, Telugu films or reporting of women's issues in Indian press. These specific studies help to raise many general questions of global significance and make a significant contribution to the contemporary critical debates on women and media.

The first part of this volume, **'Media and Gender (In)Justice'** is concerned with issues such as gender sensitization and gender policy especially in the context of media globalization. The essay by Ammu Joseph, "Wanted: A Gender Perspective on Media Globalization", traces the hazards of gender inequality in media globalization and argues how it is important for women to be figured at both the macro and micro level in the functioning of media organizations. R. Amritavalli in her essay, "Media Texts by Women for Women", places the responsibility on the women writers of media texts to create much more substantial roles for women in the television serials, releasing representations of women from the crippling confines of stereotypes. New and dynamic images must be created and set in circulation in order to change the way women and their role is perceived in contemporary social structures.

"Media-ting Patriarchy" by Bala Kothandaraman and "The Endangered Gender: Images of Women in Advertisements" by Kalpana Wandrekar, focus on the major gender issues related to commodification of women and how marketplace determines the projection of women in media texts viz. advertisements. K. Durga Bhavani in her article, "Women in Visual Media: the Spectator vs. the Spectacle", probes into another gender sensitive issue, that of woman as a spectator and the spectacle. The paper highlights the anorexic body image projected by the visual media texts and examines how these images increasingly influence the 21st century young women to follow unhealthy and punishing diets. The article, by C. Mrunalini, "Two Faces of Woman on Television: Need for a Gender Policy" concludes the first part insisting on the need to have a media policy on gender. This article showcases the inconsistencies in the local TV's projection of stereotypes in soap operas on one hand and women's programmes on gender sensitive issues on the other and demonstrates how these disparate discourses collide with each other in the media space with the former capturing the primetime slots and the latter being relegated to margins.

The second part, **'Framing Women'** provides a snapshot of the issues around media's portrayal of women – from effects on body image and self-identity to ramifications in familial and personal lives. This section also looks at the economic interests behind the objectification and eroticization of women by the media as well as efforts to counter negative stereotyping. The articles in this section explore the ways in which media both limit and empower women in society. These essays analyse a variety of media texts such as soaps, advertisements, films and news reports and address a number of issues related to representation of women in media as well as handling of women's issues in media. In her article, "Images of Women in Indian Soap Operas", Waheeda Sultana analyses how Indian soaps continue to circulate the stereotypes created by patriarchy and abound in unrealistic and implausible episodes.

The essays on film attempt to build up an awareness and understanding of how patriarchy and male gaze structure media representation of women. In the essay, "'People Said I Created Pornography': Sexuality, the Gaze and Rituparno Ghosh", Somdatta Mandal examines Indian films in the light of Laura Mulvey's central argument on male gaze and visual pleasure. Similarly, C. Vijayasree in her essay, women's Issues in Telugu Films: Limits of Social Reform" tracks the trajectory of woman-centred films in Telugu and examines the ideological underpinnings of these texts. The article highlights the discursive shifts in the genre and demonstrates that these have made no qualitative difference to the perception and handling of women's issues. The third essay on films by Shree Deepa, "A case study of the Real-life 'Wimin' in *Fire* and *Girlfriend*: Fruition to Miso Phallicisim from mere Feminism" critically examines: Indian feminist films *Fire* and *Girlfriend* against the background of critical issues in feminist film criticism. In the essay "Gender @ Cyberspace: Who's Online?" Lavanya Kolluri discusses the Internet as yet another media space available for the articulation of women's voices today. The essay raises a crucial critical issue – whether cyber space really provides women a virtual landscape to rediscover themselves or is it just a new medium for traditional mass cultural representations. "Women in Media: The Politics of Representation" by Soumya Garima Jaipuriyar, probes into the politics of reporting on gender issues such as crimes against women in society and illustrates how media reporting is politically motivated and manipulated.

It clearly emerges from the papers in this volume that the Indian media does not provide a balanced picture of women's diverse lives and their contributions to society in a changing world. Obviously much remains to be done with regard to the creation of a democratic space in media to ensure an active participation and just representation of women in media. This volume may offer no ultimate solutions to the problem of gender inequalities in the terrain of media but it certainly shows where women are today in their relationship with both traditional and new media. The world of media comes under the scrutiny of a gendered lens in these papers and stands exposed. If seeing the problems is in itself some solution to the problem, this volume, we hope, at least helps to that extent.

C. VIJAYASREE
K. DURGA BHAVANI

References

Mulvey, Laura. "Visual Pleasure and Narrative Cinema." *Screen* 16.3, 1975.

Ross, Karen and Byerly Carolyn M. (Ed.) *Women and Media: Internation Perspectives.* Oxford: Blackwell Publishers, 2004.

Van Zoonen, Liesbet. *Feminist Media Studies*London: Sage, 1994.

PART I

Media and Gender (In)Justice

1.
Wanted: A Gender Perspective on Media Globalisation

AMMU JOSEPH

I have been a woman in the media for about thirty years and ever since, I have been grappling in various ways with issues relating to both women **in** the media and women **and** media, both as a media practitioner and as a media watcher and, of course, as a person who is concerned about social issues in general and gender issues in particular.

My work on gender and media has been primarily related to the print media, particularly news and current affairs, but also women's magazines. However, in this article, I would like to highlight an aspect of the subject that cries out for more attention from academic researchers: the implications of media globalisation for concerns about women in/and media.

This is, of course, easier said than done, especially since it is a relatively uncharted territory. While both globalisation and media globalisation have received considerable attention from scholars and activists in recent times, the process of developing a gender analysis of media globalisation is still, evidently, a work in progress. But it is clearly a process that we all need to engage with and contribute to. It is particularly important, I think, for scholars in India – which boasts of a large, growing, influential and complex media environment – to provide a perspective on media globalisation, in general, and gender within media globalisation, in particular, from the global South.

The final report of the United Nations Expert Group Meeting on Women and Media in 2002, which Margaret Gallagher and I wrote together, pointed out that the far-reaching changes brought about by recent transformations in the global media system have "implications for women's access to the media and information as users, for women's participation in media and communication structures, and for the portrayal of women and their perspectives in media content." (http://www.un.org/womenwatch/daw/egm/media2002/index.html, 2002.)

At the moment no one seems quite sure what those implications are, although anecdotal evidence based on more or less casual observation suggests that we need to know more than we do. Perhaps the best way to proceed is to first figure out what exactly the changes and transformations are at the global level, what has brought them on, and how they manifest themselves in the national, regional and local contexts. We can then examine their impact on the kinds of issues we are all concerned about.

Understanding Media Globalisation

As a first step in my exploratory journey, I tried to find out what media globalisation was all about. According to American media scholars Edward S. Herman and Robert W. McChesney, the primary effect of the globalisation process is "the implantation of the commercial model of communication, its extension to broadcasting and the 'new media,' and its gradual intensification under the force of competition and bottom-line pressures." As they point out, "The commercial model has its own internal logic and, being privately owned and relying on advertiser support, tends to erode the public sphere and to create a 'culture of entertainment' that is incompatible with a democratic order. Media outputs are commodified and are designed to serve market ends, not citizenship needs."

German media economist Manfred Kops provides further, detailed and useful insights into the impact of globalisation on the media. I would strongly recommend his paper on "Globalising Media Markets: Benefits and Costs, Winners and Losers", the latest version of which is available online, to anyone who would like to come to grips with media globalisation, its economic and political consequences, its implications for public communication and, most importantly, what can be done to take the edge off what appears to be a more or less inevitable and possibly irreversible process at this point. I will only be touching on a few of these points here.

Incidentally, Kops' analysis is based on the broadcast sector, but I think it is applicable across media, especially in these days of convergence, when the lines between the various media sectors is becoming more and more blurred.

Kops acknowledges that, at one level, media globalisation can be a positive and legitimate strategy that brings benefits to media companies as well as their customers. This is basically because media globalisation involves the expansion of media markets, which generally results in media products becoming cheaper and more competitive.

Apart from reducing costs for consumers and increasing profits for companies, this process can also have an indirect but positive impact on the economies of the countries where such companies are based – through the creation of new jobs, for example.

However, he points out, the 'economic peculiarities' of the media give rise to trends that are not so positive, especially from the viewpoint of the citizen – as distinct from the consumer. Interestingly, the main problem with media globalisation appears to be that it tends to reduce media diversity in multiple ways.

One of the key concepts I learnt from Kops' paper concerns what he calls 'non-rivalry of consumption'. According to him, the economic potential of the media results from an economic peculiarity known as the non-rivalry of consumption. What this means is that once a master copy exists, little or no additional cost is involved in supplying the product to additional users. The flip side is that the high cost of making the first copy cannot be recovered if the audience for it is too small and, further, that the potential for high profits rises exponentially once the break-even number of readers or listeners or viewers has been reached.

In other words, financial viability increases as the audience for a product (a publication, a programme) grows. This is why media products become cheaper per unit and more competitive when markets expand in the course of globalisation.This trend obviously benefits media companies, but viewers, listeners and readers also stand to benefit – through lower subscription fees, for example.

However, Kops makes it clear that, in almost every other respect, both this trend and other aspects of media globalisation have potentially negative effects on public communication.

Media concentration

The first of these is the tendency towards concentration of media ownership, also known as media concentration. The increasing scale of the output of media companies seeking to maximise profits generally leads to a decrease in the number of companies, with fewer companies producing larger outputs (more newspaper copies, more TV programme minutes, et cetera). This process results in media concentration and conglomeration. The natural fallout of such a reduction in the number of media enterprises is, obviously, less diversity at the very source.

Apart from adversely affecting plurality in the media, concentration of ownership can be disadvantageous for consumers in several other ways. Some of these are common across industries. For example, as Kops points out, oligopolistic and monopolistic corporations can abuse their market power since competition among suppliers is weaker than in perfect markets. This can lead to higher prices and/or lower quality for media consumers.

However, concentration within the media has other implications that are not necessarily applicable to similar trends in other industries. For instance, in the media, economic power can readily translate into editorial and political power. This can obviously have several negative consequences. For example, monopolistic media companies can push unbalanced and biased opinions and coverage in order to further their own agendas and to influence public attitudes, especially in the political arena. They can also manipulate the public by promoting particular ideologies and values.

Since media globalisation tends to promote media concentration, it also intensifies the problems created by the uncontrolled – and often hidden – public and political influence of global media companies. From the Indian experience it is clear that these trends and consequences are not restricted to what we commonly understand as 'global media' but are also evident within national and regional media. We are most certainly witnessing them in the Indian media context.

Mainstream content

Globalisation of media markets generally also result in reduced diversity in media content. As Kops points out, even if media concentration and conglomeration can be prevented or, at least, mitigated through appropriate regulation, the 'non-rivalness' nature of media consumption inevitably gives rise to the dominance of 'mainstream', formulaic content.

As Herman and McChesney have observed, media globalisation is practically synonymous with commercialisation, commodification, and a culture of entertainment. So it is not surprising that the bottom line increasingly dictates content.

There is little doubt that it makes more economic sense to produce and distribute 'mainstream content'. Irrespective of the structure of the media industry and the size of media companies, such content is invariably cheaper per unit than content designed to meet the interests and needs of various 'minorities' among the audience (including audience categories that may be large in number but weak in influence – such as women).

In other words, the economies of scale are so great that it is virtually impossible for minority content designed for small or relatively marginal audience to compete with mainstream programming within the commercial model of communication – even if 'minorities' are willing to pay more for their own programming. The term 'minorities' is used here in a broader sense – to refer not just to religious minorities but other marginal or marginalised groups, including linguistic or ethnic minorities, groups with special interests or needs, groups that for one reason or another don't fit into the so-called 'mainstream' audience targeted by commercial media.

According to Kops, when media markets expand, larger audiences are generated mainly for programmes that were already popular in smaller markets – such as sports, movies, soap operas and pop music. In contrast, programmes meant for a more specific audience have few takers in the wider, globalised market. Thus globalisation intensifies the inherent tendency of the media to produce and supply 'more of the same'.

In the domestic arena this trend leads to the substitution of local content with sub-regional content and sub-regional content with national content. This tends to reduce the access of local and 'minority' audiences – including women – to content that fulfils their interests and needs, as well as the opportunity for such audience to articulate their concerns and perspectives through the media. It also leads to social and cultural homogenisation, which is clearly antithetical to diversity.

In this situation, public discourse becomes increasingly dominated by mainstream thinking and by persons and communities that favour that kind of thinking. As Kops points out, this can endanger the fairness, coherence and stability of nations, especially if national communities are segmented into sub-communities based on race or caste, religion or ethnicity, language or location, politics or economics and, of course, gender.

On the international stage it substitutes the national content of small nations with the national content of large nations, with the result that the former have little chance to put forward their news and views and the latter dominate public discourse at the regional and global levels.

We can certainly see this at the global level but also at the regional level – for example, in South Asia where the Indian media tend to dominate the region – and at the sub-regional and local levels.

Diversity as casualty

Thus, if cost efficiency is the primary positive feature of media globalisation, diversity is its main casualty: diversity in media companies and outlets, diversity in the variety of media products available to address the interests, needs and concerns of varied audiences, and diversity in the images and voices represented in the media. The resulting ascendancy of media monopolies and majoritarian mindsets, together with the preponderance of mainstream content based on the lowest common denominator, jeopardise public communication in any real sense of the term and diminish public discourse at all levels – local, sub-regional, national and international.

According to Kops, many of these malfunctions can be mitigated by appropriate regulation of the commercial media which can reduce the impact of market rules, as well as through vibrant non-commercial and non-governmental media, such as public service broadcasting and community broadcasting. But here in India things seem to be going in the opposite direction, with commercial factors increasingly influencing both private and state (supposedly public) media, and the government – which at long last has at least acknowledged people's right to community media – still putting bureaucratic hurdles in the path to enable citizens to realise that right.

I'm sure you all know that the Supreme Court of India, in its landmark judgment in the 1995 Cricket Association of Bengal vs. the Ministry of Information and Broadcasting case, made it very clear that the airwaves belong to the public.[1] However, as a recent article pointed out:

> The dominant idiom in media regulation in India ... seems to view corporate control over the broadcast spectrum as a surrogate for public ownership. Meanwhile, the public's access to the airwaves, where it is allowed, would need to be mediated through an array of bureaucratic controls – in effect reducing the principle to a nullity. (Muralidharan)

The Internet

Kops is not very optimistic about the so-called 'new' web-based and/or digital media either. He does acknowledge that by complementing and partly substituting for traditional media, they help to enable wider access to and participation in public communication. In this way they can increase the number of voices involved in public discourse and thereby increase its variety and plurality.

However, he points out that, in the long run, these new communication services also come under pressure from the kind of economic factors and rationale that threaten diversity in traditional broadcasters. He therefore believes that it is important to temper such economic forces with proper regulation – not only for the traditional broadcasting services but also for these relatively new communication services.

Herman and McChesney echo these concerns. According to them:

> The evidence suggests that the Internet and the digital revolution do not pose an immediate or even foreseeable threat to the market

---

1. In its landmark judgment of 1995, with special reference to the broadcast media, the Supreme Court noted: "The airwaves or frequencies are a public property. Their use has to be controlled and regulated by a public authority in the interests of the public and to prevent the invasion of their rights." In other words, the only legitimate role for the state in this regard is as trustees for the public. And broadcasters are allotted use of airwaves on the understanding that they will be used to serve the public interest.

> power of the media giants. In the current political climate...it is likely that the global media firms will be able to incorporate the Internet and related computer networks into their empires, while the egalitarian potential of the technology is minimised.

I think it is significant that media baron Rupert Murdoch's speech to the American Society of Newspaper Editors in 2005 was titled "The challenges of the online world".

Ground reality

Signs and symptoms of the media globalisation process are very much in evidence within the Indian media context today – early stages of media concentration (including cross-media ownership), growing ascendancy of the profit motive, dilution of the public service role of the media, abuse of market power, translation of economic power into political power, promotion of certain ideologies and values (and devaluation of others), supremacy of 'mainstream' content, increase in formulaic content, neglect of the interests and concerns of individuals, communities and groups who do not figure in the priorities of the market, absence of 'minority' voices and views from public debates and discussions, decline in public discourse in terms of both seriousness and plurality, social and cultural homogenisation, spread of a 'culture of entertainment,' and so on.

Yet, an attempt by the government of India last year to introduce media legislation that would, among other things, check the growing trend towards media concentration was vociferously opposed by the Indian media industry and the government buckled under pressure, at least temporarily. The draft Broadcasting Services Regulation Bill, 2006 –which came to public notice last July, was faulty on many counts, including its attempt to restrict journalistic freedoms. However, those were not the reasons why the government stepped back, if not down: the industry's objection to provisions relating to media ownership was clearly the deciding factor.

Indian industry groups lobbying against what were loosely referred to as 'cross-media restrictions' in the draft Bill argued that they would result in fragmentation, when consolidation is the need of the times (no pun intended). But, according to Kops, whose deconstruction of media concentration throws considerable light on the complex issue, the disadvantages of economic concentration are especially high in the media industry: "Concentration in the media sector...not only impairs economic competition, but also journalistic competition" (that is, competition between alternative ideas and opinions). He suggests that such a situation affects the public both directly and indirectly: it curtails freedom of opinion, reduces political and cultural diversity in media content, and impairs the media's ability to promote political competition and balance of power, as well as social integration.

The minority opinion in the Supreme Court's 1995 ruling was also emphatically opposed to media concentration. Pointing out that diversity of opinions, views, ideas and ideologies was essential for citizens to develop informed opinions on issues of concern to them, it stated that such plurality could not be provided by a medium controlled by a monopoly – whether the monopoly is of the State or any other individual, group or organisation. It also endorsed the view of the majority opinion that the broadcast media should be under the control of the public, as distinct from the government.

There is at present little to prevent media concentration in India other than the linguistic and socio-cultural heterogeneity of Indian society, and the fact that media houses here have traditionally been family-owned. These realities had so far ensured some diversity in both ownership patterns and organisational forms. However, there is considerable evidence that the process of consolidation is well under way. As South Asia and media scholar Robin Jeffrey has pointed out, the 2001 figures of the Audit Bureau of Circulation indicated trends towards market domination, if not monopolies, within the press.

The overwhelming dominance of two newspapers (per language) had become evident in seven of India's 13 major languages: in three of these (Malayalam, Punjabi and Tamil) the two lead papers controlled more than 80 % of the total circulation, while in another three (Assamese, Gujarati and Kannada) they controlled over 70 %, and in one (Bengali) over 60 %. In English, two newspapers accounted for nearly 50 % of the total circulation. In Telugu, there was just one dominant player, boasting nearly four times the circulation of its nearest rival.

This trend is only likely to intensify with the rise of cross-media ownership and the blurring of boundaries between old and new media, not to mention several recent developments in official media policy, which point towards a more permissive regulatory regime. Already several media houses have stakes in print, radio, television, Internet and cable operations. Although the relevant section in the draft Bill mentioned the need to prevent monopolies across different segments of the media, its provisions in this regard were confined to the broadcast sector.

Gender and Media Globalisation

The question is how gender fits into this picture. As mentioned earlier, this is a relatively uncharted territory. According to American feminist media scholar Carolyn M. Byerly, "Media conglomeration today, which has no shortage of critiques, lacks a feminist analysis, even though gender is a deeply imbedded aspect of the phenomenon." She says "it is essential for women to develop a solid cross-cultural gender analysis of media conglomeration." In her view, "The absence of gender-specific language and concerns signals an underlying problem in the (media reform) movement and provides a compelling reason for a parallel feminist movement to articulate what women need from a more democratic media system."

I think we can more or less assume that the growing trend towards media concentration and the consequent reduction of plurality and diversity in media organisations is not good news for gender equality in the media.

In the US, for example, Byerly has recently analysed Federal Communication Commission data on women and minority-owned media companies to find out whether the impression that women's ownership has declined significantly in recent years is correct or not. According to a working paper based on her recent work, "several decades of corporate conglomeration ... has seen media industries concentrated in the hands of only a few mega-industries whose boards, executives, and managers are primarily wealthy, white and male."

Her analysis confirms a small but possibly significant decline in women's ownership over a five-year period marked by conservative efforts towards the deregulation of media industries. According to FCC data, women currently own 3.4 per cent and minorities own 3.6 per cent of the total broadcast ownership in the US and its territories. She believes that the neoliberal policies that continue to push for deregulation of industries, including the media industry, in the US are further depriving those on the social margins access to the media and, thereby, a voice in public discourse and affairs.

Ownership is one thing, access is another. Again, I think we can be fairly certain that the larger the conglomerate the less accessible and open it is likely to be in terms of any intervention, including promotion of gender equality.

Similarly, I think we can more or less assume that the dominance of 'mainstream,' formulaic content which clearly militates against diversity in content and plurality of voices and views in the media is not going to promote more gender equality in the media. And here I think it is important to recognise that categories like women and men need to be further differentiated to ensure that the diversity within each is acknowledged and taken into account.

For example, as I often note, women are no longer missing from the Indian media, whether as media professionals or as subjects or even sources of news. If 'symbolic annihilation'[2] resulting in the absence of women from the news pages was the problem a couple of decades ago, the media are now replete with images of and references to women. The question today is not so much "Where are the women?" but "Who are these women?" Also, "When, where, how and why do they appear?" And who, among women, are still missing from the media? Whose concerns and needs are not being adequately addressed in the media?

Gender analysis of media globalisation

According to Byerly, the first step in the process of developing a gender analysis of media globalisation and conglomeration is to explore how women figure in both macro-level and micro-level realms of media organisations. The macro-level is associated with relations of power between men and women in media industries in terms of investment, executive-level decision-making and employment. The macro-level also

2. A term coined by George Gerbner (1972), which Gaye Tuchman (1978) applied to women's invisibility in serious news coverage, and has since been widely used to describe the ways in which media images render women invisible.

relates to media legislation and regulation. The micro-level is associated with media content, particularly the representation of women as subjects and coverage of issues relevant to women's lives.

It seems to me that many of us have so far been concentrating on the micro-level. Perhaps it is time for us to pay equal attention to the macro-level.

Let me end with a few quotes.

The first is attributed to Katerina Anfossi, a Latin American communicator: the "homogenisation that comes with (media) concentration has never been favourable to women ... women are about diversity."

The next two are by Maria Suarez Toro, a radio professional and gender/ media activist, also from Latin America – "Common sense would tell anyone that, in order to tackle globalisation's negative trends, they need to tackle media."

She also stresses the need for feminist media professionals, activists and scholars "to negotiate with the feminist movement to position 'women and media' and to remain conscious about globalisation and how it plays into the issue, heightens it or makes it invisible."

Clearly, then, it is important for us to take into account media globalisation, and the attendant tendencies towards media concentration as well as mainstream content, as we study, teach and perhaps take action on various aspects of women in/and the media. Such work is obviously important to ensure media diversity and sustainability – which in turn is necessary to ensure women's access to, participation in and fair representation in the media.

References

Byerly, Carolyn M. Questioning Media Access: Analysis of FCC Women and Minority Ownership Data, Working Report, August 2006.

Herman, Edward S and McChesney, Robert W. *The Global Media: The New Missionaries of Corporate Capitalism*. London:Cassell, 1997 and India:Madhyam Books, 1998.

Jeffrey, Robin. *India's Newspaper Revolution: Capitalism, Public Sphere and the Indian-Language Press,* 1977–97 (second edition with new introductory chapter). New Delhi: Oxford University Press, 2003.

Joseph, Ammu. "The Broadcast Bill and the Public Interest", *The Hindu*, 31 July 2006, <http://www.hindu.com/2006/07/31/stories/2006073100401000.htm> and "Sound and fury over the Broadcast Bill", *India Together*, 28 July 2006, <http://www.indiatogether.org/2006/jul/med-bcastbill.htm>

Kops Manfred. *Globalising Media Markets: Benefits and Costs, Winners and Losers.* < http://rundfunkoek.uni-koeln.de/institut/pdfs/21106e.pdf>

Muralidharan, Sukumar and Southasian, Himal. "The Shackling of Community Radio". March, 2007. <http://www.himalmag.com/2007/march/report1.htm>

Murdoch, Rupert. "The challenges of the online world". Washington DC, 13 April 2005. <http://business.timesonline.co.uk/article/0,,9071-1568961_3,00.html> <http://www.newscorp.com/news/news_247.html>

"Participation and Access of Women to the Media, and the Impact of Media on and its Use as an Instrument for the Advancement and Empowerment of Women – Report of the Expert Group Meeting". United Nations:2002.<http://www.un.org/womenwatch/daw/egm/media2002/index.html>

2.
Media Texts for Women by Women

R. AMRITAVALLI

There is an interesting contrast between the fictional portrait of women in media and the roles they play in the creation of media texts. In this essay, I shall speculate on the reasons for this divide and on ways to bridge it creatively, taking examples from television.

Women in Soap Operas

Let us consider the fictional portraits first. Much analysis of the portrayal of women in the media confines itself to the vapid and insensitive characters created for popular soap operas by poor writers (or by cynical teams of uncoordinated writers).[1] One is unsure if any of the writers of these soap operas are actually women, although there does seem to be at least one woman producer behind these serials. If we are to move away from saas-bahu and family sagas which often seem completely unreal, we need to have authentic writers who know the contexts that they are writing about – some of these may be men, but surely there would be a majority of women writers here.

---

1. One wonders if these serials and their characters are worth the critical attention lavished on them ad nauseum by academia; some of the 'feminist' critique of soap operas by media departments is itself dangerously formulaic, reminiscent of the formulaic approach to literary research in some of our universities.

This is not to say that we should not have saas-bahu sagas. The fact that they have an audience suggests the relevance of the theme.[2] Human relationship is the broad area of the soap opera – human relationships rooted in local realities. Infidelity, loss, honour, society, family – these are also the themes of the great classic novels. Just as in the nineteenth century, Sir Walter Scott and Charles Dickens created classics by writing in installments for journals, in a medium that was very new for its time, today, it is possible to imagine television as providing a context for producing enduring drama with its roots in the ground. What is shabby in current television is the treatment these themes receive. Surely this is an arena women should step into, or else it is an opportunity lost.

Some years ago we watched a Japanese serial centered around a child called Oshin who starts out as a very poor child worker and then grows up to pursue a profession in the city. The sustained portrayal of the life of a Japanese girl child and later a young woman was perceived by many of us as authentic and extremely interesting. The circumstances of Oshin's life were strikingly similar to those of many girl children in our own country. But we have no Indian counterpart to Oshin on television.

The arena of creative writing is relatively a matter of chance and talent; nevertheless, the greater the opportunities and the better the training, the greater the chance of the emergence of talented creative writing. Creative writing is to an extent a teachable discipline. The construction of a plot, for example, can and should be taught to many of our scriptwriters. Our audience as well, one might add, ought to be given an insight into plot construction if they are to become discerning viewers who are able to see what is missing in some of our cinematic productions. My experience in teaching scripting for radio and television shows that while some students have a natural flair for plot construction, others need to be sensitized to the elements and flow of a story – the build up, the crisis and the resolution.

There must already exist many good texts, waiting to be discovered and adapted for television. Apart from R.K. Narayan, I cannot think of any literary texts that had featured on television, that portrayed women in a

---

2. Nor are popularity and social relevance always mutually exclusive. See Waldfogel's (2007) report on a study by Jensen and Oster, which suggests that women's attitudes to girl children, wife beating and decision making – as well as behavioural patterns related to these areas – changed over a two-year period of soap opera viewing, to reflect the perceived values of their new televised peers.

sensitive and realisitic way, and raised questions of any depth about the choices they make. Yet there surely are, and have been, a number of good women writers in this country. However, if women in television fiction are still largely missing, whether as writers or as characters, it may be due to neglect, similar to what women writers suffered at the hands of the mainstream literary establishment, until very recently.

Women as Creators of Media Texts

On the other hand, women *have* entered the media as creators of media texts, although comparatively less attention has been paid by media watchers to their hard-fought battle. The opening up of the media as a serious and challenging career option for women is relatively recent. Women are now found in the arenas of politics and current affairs, investigative reporting, sports and economics to name the obvious fields. We can easily recollect women whose names we associate with these fields, and whose contribution we evaluate. Women face the camera as presenters, reporters, weather forecasters and interviewers. More jobs are opening up for them in these areas. But while considering and applauding these facts, we must ask what might motivate the vast gap between the fact and the fiction about women in the media. Why don't most of the women in current television fiction look anything like these women who work in and with television?

Could it be that this gap mirrors a cultural divide between an upper crust and the 'others' among the women in India? Notice that many of the names that spring readily to mind when we consider professional women in the media are from English-educated, middle class backgrounds. It may be too harsh to say that they seem to be doing a man's job better than a man. But this is just a dramatic way of asking what special strengths, if any, women in the media profession have brought to the media, or can bring to the media. Are there no such gender-specific special strengths? I would think there are. In managerial jobs and in the corporate world more generally, for instance, women are credited with better 'soft skills' of negotiation, and better emotional intelligence in people management. Again, women are supposed to be better at multi-tasking. So I don't think it is sexist if we acknowledge that women can bring a different outlook and a different set of strengths to their job. In other words, instead of showing that we too can do things that men have traditionally done, in the spirit of "women's cricket" or "women's tennis" or "women's hockey", perhaps we should ask what we would do if we were to approach the medium afresh, as women, without having had an agenda set for us by men. What can television by women do for women?

Television as a Vehicle for Mobility

How can television impact the lives of women in India? Let us go back to 1982, the year of the IX Asian Games in Delhi. We had not yet entered the era of satellite television, which began with the telecast of the Ramayana on Sundays – the Asiad was a precursor to those nation-wide telecasts. We were in the era of local telecasting with specific hook-ups to Delhi for specific programmes like the national news. The Asian Games provided the impetus for national telecasting of popular and public events for a sustained period of time.

These telecasts impacted the world-view of many house-bound women, whether housewives or their household helps. The Asian games provided an opportunity for community viewing during the mid-morning and the mid-afternoon. They were comparable in their impact to the Saturday movie on Doordarshan in the 1980s and 1990s, but unlike the movies, they provided not a fantasy world, often cheaply conceived, but a world of real possibilities in real settings. Delhi—the Rashtrapati Bhavan, Parliament, and the National Stadium – became a part of women's socio-political consciousness.

I recall an incident at a small school for girls who worked as maidservants. While discussing a text entitled "They have long legs", which began by speaking of an insect, and went on to speak of a bird, and an animal, they were able to anticipate that the text would mention the giraffe. These children had never actually seen one, and they had never been to the zoo. But they had seen a part of a programme on television that spoke about the giraffe – perhaps at a house where they worked!

These experiences suggest that *television is the major medium for the 'edutainment' or 'infotainment' of people with limited mobility*. By limited mobility we are to understand *limited economic mobility* as well as *limited physical mobility*. Notice that this, by and large, is still the profile of the majority of women in our country. If we fill our programmes with myth and fantasy – whether that fantasy is sanctioned by the authority of religion, or whether it is the product of male visions of the family that are simultaneously weak and sentimental, yet authoritarian, – this is what these women will imbibe. If on the other hand we try to make programmes which are relevant to their lives without being preachy, we shall be using the medium in an empowering way. It is a common experience in urban settings that poor people who have no permanent shelter and barely two meals a day will invest their money in a television set, often attracting criticism from more fortunate ones about their budgetary priorities. It may be that there is some measure of self-indulgence in their purchase of a television set. But it also shows their hunger to be a part of a larger world. What is the nature of this larger world that television can offer our women?

An Experiential Approach to Programming

We need to bring more reflection and information-sharing into many of the common areas that impact ordinary people's lives. This applies to both factual programmes or 'faction', and fiction. I will be discussing 'faction' first.

Take the education and health of our children. We now have on TV, targeted programmes for health, where the expert speaks to the common person on specific problems we may or may not have; and we have 'educational' programmes that aim to teach. These are targeted, focused, expert-oriented, often condescending, top-down programmes. But we do not have general programmes that speak to mothers and fathers about some ideas in educational philosophy or educational psychology in a language of experience that they can understand and relate to. Has anyone seen a programme, for example, on why we don't want to burden the preschool child with entrance tests, or a heavy school bag? Entrance tests were in the news a while ago, but there was no attempt to explain or understand why there were people who objected to them. If we tried to make such a programme, we would naturally speak about the stages of growth, both physical and mental, of a child; so Piaget and Montessori would enter the programme, not for their own sake, but in answer to a very simple problem that concerns all of us.

One sees this kind of a 'quest' programme sometimes on Discovery and sometimes on National Geographic. Travel and wildlife programmes that are set in India have indeed emerged. But socio-cultural-psychological programmes pertaining to life in India are yet to be seen. To continue, our imaginary programme may go on to discuss the nature of pre-school and primary school education in general, and the nature of language education, in a non-prescriptive way. One could present actual samples of classrooms, teachers, children and parents, and let viewers decide what they want for their children. At present the world of the school is a mysterious and troubled promised land for the first-generation learner, who is caught between the blind faith of the parent in an English medium education, and the scepticism bordering on contempt for a teacher who relies overmuch on parental help to get through the school year.

One could then go on to discuss what makes education relevant and non-alienating. One can imagine programmes comparing the kinds of life that a child of a given age has. What is a ten-year old child's life like in a fishing community, a weaving community, in an urban landscape? These are the kinds of questions the medium is adept at answering, for television is a great medium for conveying experience. It conveys knowledge through experience. (Hence the name 'faction'.) Some communication students once undertook a project entitled "A Day in the Life of ...," using only a handycam. Depending on whom they chose as their subject, they explored very different worlds: the world of a tour guide, of a stray dog that had been adopted by a locality, of foreign students in our country, of a woman who worked as a cleaner and housekeeper in a ladies' hostel. In such programmes, we look through the lens into the lives of people who live in different worlds; and get inducted into their sphere of knowledge.

A Fiction Rooted in Reality

Out of such research and knowledge-based faction might emerge good fiction rooted in contemporary realities. For it is when fiction has no roots in reality that it becomes inane. The best fiction – including fantasy – is that which makes us cry out in recognition, "Yes, yes, that's how things are, that's how I feel ... that's true." The truth of fiction is no less valid than the truth of science. Great fiction is great experiential truth; but just as in science there is a routine, normal, pot-boiling science; there is in fiction a routine, normal, pot-boiling variety of which we ask that it at least attain the level of superficial, 'factual' credibility. Some generations ago, for example, it was normal for Hindi cinema to portray the act of blood donation as a self-sacrificial act of suicidal proportions. This may have had its origin in a putative folk belief, captured in the following report about two Vietnamese 'boat children'[3] of the 1970s. One fell seriously ill; the other's blood group matched, and he was requested for a donation. After a period of inexplicably serious silence, he agreed, and remained in an unusually somber mood until the donation was complete; at which time his questions revealed that he believed the quantity of blood in his body to be fixed, a reservoir whose depletion would lead to his own demise. (This story of a little boy's heroism was hailed in the American media of the day.) Today, for the sake of better public knowledge and the desirability of blood donation, this fantasy about blood donation thankfully finds no place in our fiction.

Fiction, in a society that takes its knowledge-base seriously would then, steer clear of such absurd figments of the imagination, and importantly, of superstition. It would attain a level of seriousness, comparable to competent detective fiction or good science fiction, where the audience would expect internal, logical coherence in the plot and the characterization. A reader of Agatha Christie, for example, is impressed with the factual accuracy with which she depicts poisons and their effects; once we read Christie, we have left behind the world of Puck or even of Hamlet or the Romans, where mysterious substances poured into ears or eyes or noses have equally mysterious effects that the writer wants us to take on trust.

Today's detective fiction in English, on the other hand, shows meticulousness and care in its attention to factual detail. We did see a glimmer of such fiction on Indian television, in Vyomkesh Bakshi. Admittedly, this may not be great literature. But there is something to be said for quantities of competent and credible literature—a space which seems vacant today in our media. Analogously, our civilization has produced its great people – great thinkers, writers, scientists, musicians, cricketers – but often fails to ensure the competency of a large mass of ordinary people who do their jobs reliably and well. Our classical music, for example, showcases the creativity of the individual genius rather than

3. At the end of the Vietnam war, there was a phenomenon of people fleeing their country in small boats, setting sail for America.

the practiced perfection of an orchestra. The members may be individually very competent but fall short of collective brilliance. Our cricket rides on the shoulders of a few masters rather than on eleven dedicated players of adequate caliber.

A Team of Competent Players

Television is, above all, team work. This then, should be the watchword for women in media: the building up of teams who can share knowledge, and a vision arising out of that knowledge, both among themselves and with the viewer. Knowledge here would occur in a context of relevance and interest to the viewer. Such a programme would begin with a simple question that a viewer had, or a simple choice that the viewer had to make, and meander like an intelligent conversation or discussion through the pros and cons of various choices. It would not prescribe a choice necessarily; rather it would describe and explore the consequences of particular choices, and the motivations for them. Where appropriate, it would acknowledge and validate the kind of experiential knowledge that 'uneducated' or 'illiterate' women in our country possess. Let us take two examples, one of invalid knowledge, the other of valid knowledge. A pickle starts to go bad, perhaps because someone has introduced an unclean spoon into it. A maid who has helped cut the lemons worries that the cause of this could be that she had had her period at that time. This is a typical example of the imposition of a male worldview on a very natural female physiological phenomenon.

Now consider the contrasting scenario. A lady is being interviewed as a nursemaid for a patient with Alzheimer's dementia. Doctors tell us that such people tend to be very aggressive. The lady being considered for the job does not know the term Alzheimer's dementia; she is told that the person to be taken care of has a memory loss that has occurred with old age. Surprisingly, she asks: "Does this person also lose her temper frequently for no good reason?" She has understood from her experience and observation what an educated but inexperienced person possesses as theoretical knowledge.

This is the woman, then, for whom I would wish to make programmes, and whose knowledge I would draw upon for making programmes. Such women have shown resilience and courage in the face of adversity, they wear their knowledge lightly and go about their work cheerfully. What can we share with them that they would both enjoy and learn from? If the women in the profession today can share, reflect on and explore what we know about human beings, they might be able to build bridges with the vast majority of women who keep their families going in this country. For this, we need women in the media who ask questions about motives and reasons, and who stay with a subject long enough to understand it, defying the famous two-minute logic of the television byte. For example, we were once told that a father had beaten up a reluctant bride who was his daughter; the next week we were told that the daughter had agreed to the marriage, and that "all's well that ends well." The story was told by a woman reporter; and it is to her credit that she followed up the story at all. But it would be to all our credit as women if she could be supported by a team that looked much deeper into the very real mixture of problems – of violence, of choice and independence, and of immaturity and selfishness, that perhaps underlie this 'simple' story. And the understanding and insight into women's lives gained from this 'story' may lead to the creation of true fiction.

The media have a tendency to rest content with easy formulae. This is of course true of soap operas, but it is also true of the so-called serious or politically correct commentator. The formula here seems to be: the rights of the underprivileged must be protected – the poor, the minorities, women – in the way prescribed by political theory. But the media deals primarily with people, and people are complex beings. The great writers have shown us the futility of making facile and easy pronouncements on people, rich or poor, privileged or not. Much more creative talent needs to flow into television programming if the portrayal of women in it is to verge upon the reality of our lives.

Reference

Waldfogel, Joel. "TV is good for you, if you are a woman in rural India, at least." SPAN, November/December 2007.

3.
Media ting 'Patriarchy'

BALA KOTHANDARAMAN

"Because I'm worth it!"! This punch-line for a TV (and print media) advertisement, uttered in a very confident tone by a 'reigning beauty' of our times, endorsing a high-priced imported range of cosmetics, encapsulates many aspects of what the media has come to represent. It has an obvious visual-cum-celebrity appeal, wide reach, and is tapping 'aspiration'-al (a clichéd word by now) desire among the target audience; the impact it makes, reinforces the fact that the media is 'objectifying', 'stereotyping', 'commodifying' women, the feminine, female sexuality, and so on.

This paper attempts to go a little beyond this litany of charges nailing the media for perpetuating patriarchy. The objective of the paper is to contextualise what appears to be an 'unstoppable' phenomenon and to interrogate the place of feminist theory in all this. A brief appraisal of critiquing media portrayal will be followed by a postulate to understand the role played by the interplay of the 'two economies' involved.

The dominance of the media, particularly that of the technological media, appears 'unstoppable' as the communication industries are proving to be among the most lucrative of all avenues, generating profits in mind-boggling numbers world-wide. In India, as consumers, we are witness to the astonishing rise of communications technology and the related entertainment industry. These have certainly resulted in more employment opportunities, more revenue and given the electronic media's obvious control over its own hype, the whole thing has 'come of age' – a recurrent cliché which translates into appreciating all the programmes/products which are closely modelled on everything that is the current rage in the West. And this includes the portrayal/role of women.

The first point which I wish to debate is that in an era where there is considerable awareness on empowerment of women, and the ire raised by continued 'objectification' of women by the media, how is it that innumerable protests have no impact? Every time a protest is made, there is a flurry of media attention; occasionally, a show of 'concern' expressed by some public authority—and soon, its back-to-business – the business of nonchalantly reinforcing palpably unacceptable gender stereotypes. Business: that's the keyword!

The players involved in the Business are the producers/promoters, the audience – the public in general. The first set rake in the profits hence brickbats do not hurt them. They pass on the responsibility, when cornered, to 'audience preferences' bolstered by TRP and other ratings (all these are debatable criteria), and the public in general is almost indifferent to any serious issues; be it gender, environment, elections, democracy... in fact, in the flush of all-round commercial success, any protesting voice is derogatorily termed 'feminist'. Nothing sells cricket so well as Mandira Bedi as anchor (and never mind the adverse reactions of all those who know the game or of people, especially women, who refute the spiel trotted out that Bedi draws in/represents women's interest in the sport). Woman as eye-candy, to use the already-clichéd current terminology, has become entrenched in all the media.

How is that the women involved (models, personnel in ad agencies/print or electronic media) arguably the most important players of the lot, acquiesce in this systematic derogation, and play the lead in re-establishing all the gendered stereotypes? A matter of noted interest is that this is a bunch of educated, articulate young women from well-to-do backgrounds who certainly do not typify the pre-women's rights era kind of home-bound, suppressed, oppressed and exploited women who need to be liberated. (Equally, the male personnel also come from similar backgrounds and are expected to be more gender-sensitive).The clue to their compliance lies in commercial success; the 'good money' (pun intended) that they make, along with 'value-added' publicity and fame. Aspirational careers in movies override all the inhibitions of their (largely) middle-class upbringing. It should also be added that the current general societal milieu enables such aspirations – the disapproval of an earlier decade, the parental frown, the social stigma on anything other than higher studies/ respectable career options has gradually thinned. In most cases parents and other 'elders', while using 'the vulgar display in the media' as a conversation-piece, acquiesce through politically correct silence (they do not want to be perceived as old-fashioned), and in certain cases parents become managers of their daughters' upward spiralling career and wealth (frequently giving up their own staid careers). They don't seem to squirm with embarrassment while their little girls 'bare-all and dare-all' when lavish sums of money pour in.

The hype generated through the media is that these are 'modern, liberated women' ready to flaunt their 'beauty' and their bodies in their competition to 'expose', and to project 'attitude'. The image they project is precisely the opposite of what the truly modern woman i.e., one who evolves into a person in terms of ideas, capability, individuality, stands for; this Media-ted 'modern' creature is ironically a throwback to the woman-as-object Stereotypically Feminine. One wonders whether this is what women's liberation is all about! Specialists in the field of media need to conduct a study on this phenomenon of distortion of terminology, a clear case of subversive language-politics wherein, any imitation of western modes such as 'cat-walking the ramp' is praised as India's fashion industry having 'come of age'.

What does this scenario mean in terms of theory? For clearly, it does not fit in with classic Patriarchy which Feminism of the 1970s had challenged. The Media-ted woman has, so goes the spiel, stepped out into the world, is facing it on her own terms, is unhindered by all the old restrictions on her female being; she claims, in hackneyed publicity interviews that this mindless, bimbette behaviour highlights her femininity. Clearly, a far more complex power-structure is at work re-entrenching traditional Patriarchy albeit in a new avatar, the Patriarchy that had been earlier challenged in a meaningful way. To illustrate my point, let me take up two terms made familiar by Feminism: internalisation and complicity.

'Internalisation' posits that women, in patriarchical hierarchy, acquiesce in their subordination because of:

- Their biology, physique, et cetera
- Their being less intelligent
- Their lack of knowledge of the world

They therefore have to depend on the Master Male. This situation has been universally accepted for centuries.

Questioning and dismantling this structure propelled Women's Lib and Feminism, giving woman her individuality as a thinking being – a transformation visible in, and accepted by society in the later 20th Century.

Now let us interrogate 'modern' Media-ted representation: we find that it endorses directly or subtly the same Internalisation as above:

- Women signal beauty, 'Bod', et cetera
- In advertisements, in TV serials, women are often dumbed down
- Educated, 'working' women too lack a knowledge of the world

And often, their whole endeavour is to titillate/captivate/get the approval of the male.

So Where is the Change?

The difference is in the presentation – the Media-ted Internalisation is done via glitz, glamour, smart 'copy', and thus camouflages what is actually status quo.

'Complicity' in feminist theory holds that under Patriarchy, women accept/ endorse subordination because of

- A lack of alternative
- Resistance to being futile
- An in-built comfort zone
- They are the nominal power behind the throne

The Women's Movement has gone a long way in dismantling this structure and changing societal gender attitudes in the later 20th Century.

However, as Media representation persists in reinforcing status quo stereotypes, we need to interrogate the 'Complicity' paradigms:

- Is there really no alternative?
- Why is resistance futile in a milieu of so much awareness?
- Has money/fame, the outcome of commercialisation, become the new 'Comfort Zone' overriding traditional inhibitions?

- Where is the change in attitude with the Media-ted glamour woman being hyped as 'Woman Power' vis-à-vis the traditional patronizing label of woman as 'power behind the throne'?

Once again, the difference is in the presentation – the glamour, glitz, and money of Media-ted representation camouflage the re-entrenching of old stereotypes and gender roles.

In a visibly consumerist environment, raising these questions results in the questioner being labelled/condemned as old-fashioned, moralist and/or 'Feminist'.

Is it therefore advisable to throw up one's hands and let long-entrenched Patriarchy flourish albeit in this new garb? Surely not! How then do we understand/contend with this phenomenon? I posit that our approach has to make certain necessary shifts, as it is clear that the current scenario is far more complex than can be countered by merely protesting about 'derogatory representation of women' or about manifestations of clear-cut patriarchy in the traditional sense.

The altered perspective we need to bring in has to keep in mind two features of the situation. First, that two economies are actually in operation; and second, that the dialogistic resonances set up by the enmeshing of these two call for critical attention as a monologic approach has become inadequate.

The two economies referred to are the Financial and the Cultural.

The Financial: The foregoing discussion has highlighted the materialistic attraction of Media-ted impact which is drowning out the earlier societal norm that 'money is not everything'. In an era in which technological progress has made global communication instantaneous and reasonably cost-effective, the rapid circulation, replication and distribution of all types of information (news, educational material, business information, weather, movies, music) has become the order of the day. Circulating all of this as a business venture so as to make profit calls for planned marketing: in other words, a financial economy comes into place as with any commodity, and the environment becomes competitive.

The Cultural: Technological progress has also ushered in Mass Culture; the McLuhanesque global village is a reality. Entertainment/ Pop culture has become a commodity; technological progress has rendered this cultural commodity easy to replicate and distribute (although initial production costs may be high); sophisticated marketing makes it a profitable venture inviting more players/competitors. Initial criticism notwithstanding, the glamour and the glitz, the lure of fame and monetary success draw in participants. Claims are then made that this is what 'the people'/audiences want. Cultural commodity in the process of being marketed reveals a peculiarity: it in turn becomes a producer. It produces an audience; and this audience, in turn, is sold to advertisers or sponsors. The advertisers or sponsors market lifestyles, attitude, aspirations and entice/draw in larger sections of the populace including the hitherto conservative, value-conscious middle classes. This is the resultant *cultural economy*.

Let us take the examples of cricket commentary, or cosmetics, both of which have been around for decades. For long, print, radio and thereafter black-and-white TV cricket commentary provided information and excitement about the game and talented players; the entry of colour and satellite television has commodified the whole gamut of 'stakeholders' along the path outlined above, such that cricket commentary is now an economy on its own; as a cultural economy it has colluded with financial economy to 'object-ify' women.

Cosmetics, a traditional feminine item derided as 'make-up' acquired 'niche' status for certain expensive brands (particularly foreign ones) in a financial economy. Media-ted beauty contests and/or fashion shows, especially following a run of Indian Miss World/Universe winners have transformed the whole thing into successful cultural economies. (Also note that the opposition to beauty contests has died down as the cosmetics/ fashion industry has captured the huge middle class market and has created aspiration in Tier II cities and smaller towns, spawning wannabe contests in such locations as well).

The cultural economy has similarities with the financial economy but it is more complex in that it has to keep on generating its own hype and constantly offer innovations to keep afloat and to beat competition (a possible reason why we keep hearing 'as far back as two years/six months ago' over the media: the shelf life of social (media-ted) memory keeps getting shorter).The two economies obviously interact; the growing money-power generated through the IT and BPO industry provides an economic avenue through which India's media-ted industry impacts GenNext—and their parents enabling them to enter a new sphere of consumerist spending and acquiring life-styles which give them the 'feel-good' effect. This achievement of becoming 'mod' nullifies, in relevant contexts, 'the cussed' Feminist voices.

It is obvious that big financial players influence the current media world, and women's role in this regard calls for a separate study. The one instance in the Indian context, Ekta Kapoor, unfortunately promotes and celebrates the worst aspects of retrograde stereotypical patriarchy via her soaps – which reify cultural economy as financial economy, and the producer remains unmoved by criticism of her disregard of the medium's social responsibility.

To move on to the second aspect, namely the dialogistic resonances. The concept of 'the people' who constitute the audience cannot remain a monolithic one, particularly when it relates to the production and consumption of technologically mediated (popular) cultural commodity. Different segments react in different ways, providing one more role-shift whereby each segment of audience-as-commodity/consumer becomes producer of meanings/pleasures. Aware that informed criticism can hurt their financial economy, producers of cultural commodities are anxious to bridge the gap between varieties of reactions – more particularly, to package and market the product and target audience effectively so that resistance can be worn down/ worn out – a major reason why the old battle-cry of 'patriarchy' proves inadequate in the current scenario.

For instance, there is the veneer of gender equality when male models, Mr Gladrags contests, metrosexuals, men's beauty/grooming parlours are also promoted and form flourishing business ventures. The glamour our girls and boys, their lifestyles, dialogues, their very appearance acquires a westernised veneer in the name of globalisation; anything Indian about them is marketed, expensively, as 'ethnic'. Look beneath the surface and all the old stereotypes of gender roles and behaviour persist: that is the media-ted cultural economy at work! Take for example, the commodification of Karva Chauth (a tradition whose practice women's consciousness groups argue against), or wedding extravaganzas. In a nutshell, triviliasation is the name of the game!

Hence this paper suggests that it is necessary to address the strengths of heteroglossic discourses in the formulation of our theoretical constructs in the attempt to dismantle media-ted patriarchy rather than merely lambast classical patriarchy. This would mean addressing the sub-texts of contesting/contending subtleties of late capitalism which the globalised media in its depiction of women reinforces retrogressively in a nonchalant manner: these can be addressed by paying attention to the dialogistic implications of resistance modes.

That is to say, Resistance needs to recognize that there are two main forms of social power – namely, the power to construct meanings, pleasures, social identities (which is a largely semiotic power) and the power to construct a socioeconomic system (a largely social power). Resistance modes should correspond to each or both of these as the situation warrants; for instance, by drawing in the Media-ted young women (and men) as well as students in a participatory mode. (Could they be made to realise that "such-and-such product should be worthy of me as sentient human" rather than 'Because I'm worth it!' as a commodified Media-ted creature would pout it?)

At the level of conceptualization, Resistance implies re-formulating theory to accommodate the post-feminist context. As semiotic intervention, it calls for dialogistic engagement with the Indian demographic profile of the world's largest number of young people below the age of 25; with an urban-rural divide in terms of opportunities and aspiration created by media's reach; with rural market-penetration by MNCs and large corporates; with a range of regional languages whose individualities are being eroded and forced into a globalised media-ted English/Hindi/Hinglish. These are the targets of a globalised socio-economic system (the social power) which the media aims at constituting, and it is they who need to be made aware of the pitfalls.

Postscript 1: In the interim between the Seminar and this publication of the Papers presented, a major new event has taken centre-stage: the IPL. This game is noticeably electronic media-centric, and readily fits into the paradigm of the 'two economies' discussed above. In particular the introduction of the cheerleaders exemplifies the open-eyed, deliberate commoditisation of women in this version of media-ted cultural economy stimulating the financial market economy.

Postscript 2: A classic example of subversion of language and terminology clearly intended to reify patriarchy in all its stereotypes, indicative of attitudes within media houses coming as it does from a well-known senior journalist:

The Temperature in Murree

While the proliferating Pakistani 24x7 news channels may not be a patch on ours, their female newscasters and anchors are prettier. Before I get lynched (some of my best friends are anchors!), let me add that the ladies of Lahore are prettier only in the male chauvinist sense. Our girls, undeniably, are brainier and sharper, but they lack oomph!

Vinod Mehta, (Ed.), *Outlook*: 6 April, 2009 in "Delhi Diary".

Note

This Paper acknowledges John Fiske, "The Popular Economy" in John Storey, (Ed.), *Cultural Theory and Popular Culture: A Reader* (N.Y., Prentice Hall: 1998) for the input of the 'two economies'. (The 1998 edition was published by University of Georgia Press).

Its application to and the reading offered in the Indian context is my own.

4.
The Endangered Gender: Images of Women in Advertisements

KALPANA WANDREKAR

The global review observation of 1980 states, "A consistent picture emerges from those research studies which have investigated the media's portrayal of women. At the very best, the portrayal is narrow; at worst it is unrealistic, demeaning and damaging." (Gallagher, 1981)

Media has erased the geographical distances and is now an integral part of man's living space. The impact of visual media as well as print media on the mind of the viewers and readers is tremendous. This necessitates looking into the coding and construction of femininity and whether or not it reflects reality. This essay will attempt to examine the images of women in newspaper advertisements and television commercials.

We often feel that there exists a disparity between women's actual lives and their representations in the media. This disparity exists, as the images of women in media seem to be a male fantasy and not a living reality. It is therefore necessary to understand how media constructs femininity. In the book, *Affirmation and Denial: Construction of Femininity on Indian Television* (1990), Prabha Krishnan and Anita Dighe refer to the complexity of women and media interaction, which is an outcome of the production of self-consciousness by media and society. Media as an organization seems to consolidate patriarchal ideology and define femininity. Decoding the content by analyzing images, is an attempt to question that ideology, which has commodified women and stereotyped them.

As recorded by the 1995 Beijing conference on women, article 236 reads "the continued projection of negative and degrading images of women in media communications – electronic, print, visual and audio – must be changed. Print and electronic media in most countries do not provide a balanced picture of women's diverse lives and contributions to society in a changing world..." Programmes that reinforce women's traditional roles can be equally limiting. The world-wide trend towards consumerism has created a climate in which advertisements and commercial messages often portray women of all ages, inappropriately and primarily as consumers and target girls. It was in the same year that Indian NGOs appealed to halt the commodification of the female body.

Advertising becomes a cultural institution as it mirrors the mores and norms of behaviour in the society. Social mores keep changing, usually growing more and more liberal. Advertising is about appearances and about product information. While giving product information, advertisement creates an appearance of the product which converts an object or product into an idea. This happens through the advertiser's skill at positioning the product through an image. By being an ideological narrative, advertisements send subtle messages about those ideologies which are endorsed and propagated by the dominant structure of patriarchy. A historical perspective will show the evolution of this ideology.

The history of advertising in India records the appearance of the first advertisement in *Hickey's Bengal Gazette*, India's first newspaper. In 1912, ITC launched Gold Flake. In 1939 Levers launched Dalda and marketed it as an exclusive brand .This was the beginning of strategizing, planning and branding a product. Lux, started using a celebrity, actor Leela Chitnis, in 1941, to endorse their soap. Advertisements came to the radio in 1967 with the first commercial aired on Vividh Bharati. Commercial TV advertisements began in 1976 and the first coloured TV commercial of Bombay Dying appeared in 1982. Advertising at the beginning, was mostly meant for information and not for promotional purposes.

In 1972, the United Nations Commission on the Status of Women noted that in all its efforts to promote the advertisement of women, it had encountered a serious obstacle in the deep-rooted attitudes of men and women which tended to perpetuate the status quo. The Commission also observed that those attitudes were due to cultural patterns which, to a great extent, determined thoughts and feelings about women and men. These in turn were being disseminated on a vast scale as a result of technical advancements in mass communication and media.(UN Expert Group Meeting on Women and Media, Vienna 1981.)

The same year on 25 March 1972, in *Blitz*, a weekly magazine, a woman's photograph was shown titled 'Women's Lib.' with a few lines which read "If she wants to wear a little, you must let her wear a little or, perhaps, she'll wear a lot." This ditty does not apply to Kelly Anne Page, an actress who believes that a woman can and should wear anything she wants in this age of Women's Lib. But in general images of women in advertisements of that time look very sober.

Around this time, sure enough a change did occur in the way both men and women perceived a woman's body. To illustrate some of the points let us look at some advertisements.

Images of Women in Print Media

I have analysed some advertisements from different newspapers and magazines such as *The Times of India*, *Asian Age*, *Indian Express* and *Blitz*.

An issue of the 'Pune Times' (*The Times of India*, 2 Sept. 2004) shows a picture of Penelope Cruz, a Hollywood actor from the ultimate food film *Woman on Top* lying on a bed of red chillies and her body covered by red chillies. Here the woman's body seems to appear as a dish for consumption. The red colour of the chillies signifies passion. According to Goffman, the figure of a woman on a sofa is a "conventionalized expression of sexual availability."

Another advertisement 'Dating Sutra' appeared in 'Pune Times' (*The Times of India*, 31 Jan. 2007). Like 'Raslila', it announces, 'Date-lila is here. Choose your date from a range of profiles'. The words 'sutra' and 'lila' signify religious sanction as the man at the center obviously suggests Sri Krishna and 'Raslila' is taken from Hindu mythology. The illustration shows six beautiful women with a man in the middle holding a mobile. The background is of a beautiful garden with banana trees, creepers full of white flowers, peacocks, parrots and a black bull – all romantic signifiers with erotic suggestions. The man looks real whereas the women look unreal as in paintings. This is what Goffman calls "ritual of subordination". Again it's a male fantasy and perception of women.

Are women endangered by such images? As advertisements are visual constructs, 'seeing' becomes an important factor of analysis. Art critic John Berger writes "men look at women. Women watch themselves being looked at. This determines not only most relations between men and women but also the relation of women to themselves. The surveyor of women in herself is male: the surveyed female. Thus she turns herself into an object – and most particularly an object of vision: a sight." (Berger: 47) Women are constantly under male gaze which gives men voyeuristic pleasure.

Laura Mulvey in her seminal essay, "Visual Pleasure and Narrative Cinema" (Screen, 16: 6–18. 1975) observes the power of male gaze ,"in a world ordered by sexual imbalance, pleasure in looking has been split between active /male and passive /female. The determining male gaze projects its phantasm on to the female figure which is styled accordingly. In their traditional exhibitionist role women are simultaneously looked at and displayed with their appearance coded for strong visual and erotic impact so that they can be said to connote to-be-looked-at-ness."

Media largely controls the minds of the viewers' socialization processes and defines gender roles. Media not only 'reflects' but 'affects' social reality. By being selective of which 'light' in which to portray an image, media reinforces social values, attitudes and behaviour patterns. Advertisements themselves are products of a capitalistic system which uses them to sell a product. Although sometimes we come across informative advertisements which are non-stereotypes.

Images of Women in TV Commercials

Abhik Roy in his book *Selling Stereotypes* (1998), categorizes women's images into different types– women as commodities, objects to be viewed, signifiers for products, non-thinking decorative objects and fragmented objects. I believe media propagates man's idea of a woman's beauty. The images in media are often unreal and attempt to show how an ideal woman should look and behave. The suggested message is that she should satisfy man's sexual desires. The commercial onslaught persuades the viewer to believe in the make-believe images. This belief in the flawed image of the ideal woman who should be thin, is discussed by Jean Kilbourne in "Can't Buy My Love: How Advertising Changes the Way we Think and Feel" where she writes "Women learn from a very early age to spend enormous amounts of time, energy and above all money striving to achieve this ideal and feeling ashamed and guilty when we fail. And failure is inevitable because the ideal is based on absolutely flawlessness."

Many advertisements talk about how to get a fair complexion in a short time and once the girl gets it, she immediately manages to get a job as an air hostess or a cricket commentator or a model. In the advertisements of Fair and Lovely, Emami, Fair Glow, Fair One, the male gaze is attracted by the fair complexion. The transformation brought about by the cream, within three weeks, is amazing. This is how femininity gets defined. The commercials perpetuate male defined identity. These images of women who glitter in glamour also sends the message that women should do everything to be looked at because they can get success at work by being looked at. Women are used as signifiers. The woman viewer is expected to have luxuriant hair (advertisements of Vatika, Brahmi Amla), soft complexion (advertisements of Dove, Santoor) and always remain young (advertisements of Streak, L'oreal) like the models shown in the advertisements.

Emphasis is always given on beauty and body so that the cosmetic industries make business. Since women are mostly the decision makers about what to buy for a home, they are targeted as customers and also as promoters of products. The advertisements of Parle G—'G for genius' where the boy of eight induces his father's opponent to play a wrong move in a game of chess to make the father win, or the advertisement for Mentos– 'deemak ki batti jalade' in which a college student who is late to class tricks the professor by pretending that he is leaving show boys and not girls conforming to the patriarchal belief that women are unintelligent. The images of women seem to have conformed them into domesticity as they are shown doing household jobs such as cooking (advertisement of Everest masala), serving,(advertisement of M.D.H masala) scrubbing (advertisement of Wheel) and while doing these, they are shown well dressed and smiling happily. The message implies that a woman's place is inside the house so they are shown playing the roles of ideal wives, caring moms and rarely as working women.

However sometimes we do come across non-stereotypical images in commercials. A wife is served tea when she comes home from work. The ad says 'Life should have some consistency' (advertisement of Society Tea), Sharmila Tagore educating pregnant women about AIDS and a few advertisements dealing with rural life and its problems (advertisement of Sufala). However these portrayals are few and far between. These advertisements too try to emphasize that a woman's space is her home.

The Impact of Women's Images in Media

Widespread, overt depiction of a woman as a body and not a being is expected to have an impact on general beliefs and attitudes. It is agreed upon by many that sexually degrading media images of women promote rape supportive attitudes and beliefs.

The stereotypical portrayals of women can increase self-consciousness about their looks in public, persuade an acceptance of domesticity, decrease aspirations, increase the divide in genders and attempt a stereotyped definition of femininity.

The expensive jewellery and clothes, affluent lifestyles and beautiful homes shown in the advertisements widen the gap between the rich and the poor. This can cause frustration, discontent and inferiority complex.

This is how the depiction of women in advertisements and TV commercials endanger the gender through their images.

References

Krishnan, Prabha and Dighe, Anita. *Affirmation and Denial: Construction of Femininity on Indian Television.*

Goffman E . *Gender Advertisements.* New York : Harper and Row, 1987.

Berger, John. *Ways of Seeing.* London: British Broadcasting Corporation: Penguin Books, 1972.

Mulvey, Laura. "Visual Pleasure and narrative Cinema" (1975, Screen, 16, 6–18).

Kilbourne, Jean "Can't Buy My Love: How Advertising Changes the Way we Think and Feel".

Roy Abhik. *Selling Stereotypes* (1998).

5.
Woman in Visual Media: The Spectator vs. the Spectacle

K. DURGA BHAVANI

There is a basic connection between a woman's experiences in real life and a woman's experiences in visual media, which essentially forms the relationship between the spectator and spectacle. It is assumed that women are generally taught to be objects of spectacle in their everyday life and they have something in common with the image of women on the screen/visual media. The woman enters into the mediated world of film or television with a context that is structured wholly for her absence/invisibility, which of course, often mirrors her real life. Feminist film critics Laura Mulvey has said that, "The woman is not visible in the audience which is perceived as the male" and Claire Johnston observes, "The woman is not visible on the screen, as she is merely a surrogate for the phallus, a signifier for something else...."(Gamble, 79)

The visual media codes have manipulated the absence of the woman to such an extent that the limited choices allowed to her are – to identify firstly with the image of the woman (structured by the male) on the screen, secondly with the male audience sitting by her side in the theatre and finally with the heroes in the films and their super human actions. The narrative of the film places the woman spectator with the 'hero'. The emotions of the women accepting 'masculinization' (a term used by Laura Mulvey, 1975) while watching the actions of the hero are enriched by the emotions of a heroine of a sentimental comedy. This suggests that films are generally made by men and the point of reference is always entrenched in patriarchal structure. Thus, as it has been observed, this kind of 'trans-sex identification' has almost become a habit for women.

The crucial issues raised in this article are: firstly, isn't it possible for the producers of film and TV to portray more realistic images of women?

Secondly, how far is it possible for the female filmmaker to resist the projection of stereotypes and reclaim her own voice? Thirdly, to what extent can the female spectator influence the content of the visual media by correcting the traditional stereotypes?

Women's Role in Films

Despite the emergence of many ordinances against gender discrimination across the world, women are undermined in all fields media. They are given low-paid jobs when compared to the jobs offered to men. They are kept away from decision-making and any other task involving power. In support of this, a female filmmaker has remarked, "Behind every masterpiece of male intelligence are hidden women, the editors, continuity girls, script girls who are forgotten in that most incredible of all film fantasies... ." Moreover, gender as portrayed within popular media reveals that the role of women in relation to contemporary media has not changed much when compared to older media forms.

In the films of 50s and 60s especially in India, the image of the woman revolved round the concepts of love and sacrifice. Being emotional was considered to be feminine and the equivalent actions shown in films to these emotions were the household duties such as cleaning and washing. This association was extended to real life images of women in society and vice versa. As a result, the housewife, following her romantic models in the film was led on the path of love and sacrifice to the drudgery of household duties. These representations naturalized their position within the domain of household duties. Thus, the romantic model and the domestic realities were entwined in the woman-spectator's life in society, one redeeming or compensating for the other. Thus, the theme of self-sacrifice, which formed the core of Indian films penetrated into the female spectator's psyche for more than three decades since the 1950s.

This kind of romantic, self-sacrificing image of the woman in films is perhaps central to the notion of 'middleclassness' i.e., it is more a state of mind than an economic status, which is based on relatively stringent and rigid ethical codes followed in the middle class households. Women are bound to adhere to these social codes in controlling their creative urges but the same morality allows more freedom to their male counterpart in deviating from the norm. In this circumscribed world of the woman, the range of options open to her are very limited and she is cocooned in her shell. The portrayal of a woman in film as well as her role in society appears to be governed by the notion that a woman's well being and fulfillment are dependent on institutions such as marriage, family, motherhood et cetera which obviously end her independent identity. Beyond the recurring stereotypical images of women, such as self-sacrificing mother, wife, a victimized daughter-in-law, a villainous mother-in-law, there is no other way in which women are portrayed in films although they play several different roles in society. Hence, there is a wide gap between the projection of women in visual media and the women in real life. Although media projection of men's roles also suffers from stereotyping, it is not as disturbing as that of women since men have a power-wielding position in society.

Woman as Spectator

'Memory' is an important concept in the study of media audience in general and the female spectatorship in particular. Memory is not just a straightforward representation of easily accessible past events, which can be retold. It involves a set of complex psychological and cultural processes, producing identities through the negotiation of public discourses and private narratives. Many spectators of cinema have their treasured memories and their continued pleasure in recollecting the past. For example their judgment of a film is based on their act of relating the past aspects of film making to those of the present. It has been argued that the chief pleasure of such memories lie in the way they work as 'personal utopias', which offer a kind of escape from the constraints of real life. The spectators' memories of their favourite stars provide them 'utopian fantasies' which are dependent on the expectations or the unfulfilled needs and desires of their lives. Thus, both the process and the subject of the memory involve utopias of some form. For example, women's expectations of romance and motherhood may be reconstructed according to their relationship with film ideals of femininity. Feminine ideals as is often mentioned, are by definition never realizable since they fundamentally contradict each other; for example, the construction of motherhood contradicts her sexual desirability. Hence, memories of film stars are particularly significant for women spectators in terms of their 'fantasy self' never realized in real life. In this context, it is necessary to mention Janice Radway's (1984) groundbreaking theory on women's act of 'romance reading'. She argues that "The act of romance reading can be conceived as an activity of mild protest and longing for reform necessitated by those institutions' (heterosexuality and monogamous marriage) failure to satisfy the emotional needs of women. Reading therefore functions for them as an act of recognition and contestation whereby that failure is first admitted and then partially reversed..." (Radway: 213).

Viewing romance or villainy in soap operas is also a social act for many of these women as housewives. Even though, they realize the fact that the characters in all these soaps are unrealistic and do not resonate with their everyday lives, they immerse themselves in watching the stereotypes. The women spectators perhaps find it an enjoyable intervention in their domestic drudgery. Although television viewing is generally considered a social activity, which enables simultaneous conversation with family members, watching midday soaps is a private activity, which only housewives enjoy, blocking out the surrounding world. Many advertising companies come forward to sponsor the myriad episodes in the soaps which are ridiculously prolonged to cater to a majority of housewives – young, old and middle aged. This activity gives women an illusion of pleasure while their real life situation produced by patriarchy remains unchanged. The mediocrity of the story-lines of these soaps creates a totally artificial world against an illusion of the natural world.

This repetitive serial viewing among Indian middle class women is considered more an addiction than entertainment. Although the women who do not surrender to patriarchal hegemony may not necessarily identify with the stereotypes of TV soaps, they find them an aberration. Perhaps, the experience of watching the evil actions of femme fatales on the screen creates a kind of psychological satisfaction or fulfillment in some of them of protesting against patriarchal norms. The fact that these serials often do not have any value of reality encourages them to watch them more intently day after day; this is perhaps a psychic strategy by which they try to empower themselves in everyday life leaving apart their harmful consequences on society. This is an act of engaging themselves in 'utopian fantasies' of a different kind. The prolonged nature of these serials ensures the security of their pleasure in watching them regularly, which perhaps increases their desire to be entertained against the fear of vacuum that the conclusion of the serial creates in their daily routine. What is often talked about in the media is that constant viewing of TV soaps by housewives, the ideological consequences of their mass production and consumption by the women spectators has been considered a social problem in Indian middle class societies.

Women and their Body Image in the Media

Another important aspect of the unrealistic portrayal of women in media texts deals with the woman's body as a spectacle. Media is strongly criticized for reproducing and extolling representations of unrealistic female figures. As a result, young women, influenced by certain body images shown in films and advertisements, believe that being thin is beautiful. The discrepancy between media image and the real life image lead these young women to resort to undesirable ways of dieting and exercise which is viewed as a serious medical problem across the world. The dissatisfaction of body image starts almost at the age of fourteen in girls and it is often associated with disorderly eating patterns at the vital period of physical development. Film and advertisements increasingly focus on woman's looks and grooming and disproportionate body images of women are often objects of fun and ridicule. This in turn, creates artificial standards for young college girls. Worldwide surveys have produced consistent evidence that a thin body is associated with personal, professional and social success. This impression is nurtured by the media texts which may not reflect the real life situation in multicultural societies of third world countries. Thus, in almost all media texts such as films, advertisements, beauty pageants and women's magazines, the norms of feminine beauty emphasize the ideal of slender body, which the media consumers across cultures try to follow.

Thus, media creates a kind of make-believe situation by provoking non-western societies to imitate western models. These overt representations of the idealized slender female form have harmful consequences for the self-perception of women who do not see themselves as complying with the stereotypes of feminine beauty. "Certainly cultural beauty in relation to body shape is promulgated to a significant degree through visual/ verbal media texts" (Wykes and Gunter: 206). The reason for the focus on anorexic body image is that "it is women's bodies rather than any other attribute which appear to make them worthy of being represented... Women feature in media texts more often as slender and sexy. The female body is a spectacle, it is something to be looked at whether real or mediated: it is looked through in the search for female identity". (Wykes and Gunter: 206). The argument that "media causes eating disorder assumes not only that representations misrepresent but they inscribe directly women to train and shape and modify their bodies to conform to what very clearly are impossible ideals".

It is basically, the patriarchal dominance of the family that influences the media industries to represent the male ideal of female appearances and the roles of the women. Besides, it is not only the media industry that describes and determines the image of women's bodies but also other industries such as fashion, beauty, fiction and even finance, all of which are aspects of the dominant capitalist culture. Thus, the power of the image of the woman's body pervades through the cumulative impact of multiple texts across genres. Each text represents the woman on one hand as a cultural idol placed in romantic-gendered love, family, financial security and fame. On the other hand, she is seen working hard to earn money while serving the interests of multi-billion dollar industries in promoting this image. In fact, media texts represent these images of women in their advertisements, newspapers and TV shows about fashion and lifestyles.

We are increasingly made to live in a 'publicity saturated culture' which is referred to as 'information blizzard' by Baudrillard (1983). By this term, he means that in this culture, the images and the messages refer to each other rather than to any external reality. He further states that the gap between representation and reality is so significantly wide that "we are living in a society of excrescence, that is, that which incessantly develops without being measurable against its own objectives" (Baudrillard, quoted by Wykes and Gunter) Innumerable signals and messages are being produced and transmitted by the modern mass media within such a short time that they never acquire any meaning and significance for the people involved. In this process of bombarding the spectators with so many images the print and visual media across the world endeavour to sell themselves by selling sex and slenderness. Women, as a part of this business continue to feature as promoting these two aspects of femininity.

Under the impact of feminism, women's magazines from 1960 focused on women's careers and their sexual liberation in order to cater to the audience who were young, ambitious and politically well informed. But this was only a part of their business acumen or tactfulness rather than a serious commitment to women's rights and gender equality. In the

21st century, this trend of portraying women as successful and career-oriented is increasing in films and other forms of visual media but these representations are embedded in a more traditional gender narrative which focuses on the likes and dislikes of men. For example, in the films, the heroine despite being educated and career-oriented is almost always on the quest for love and her only goal is to win the heart of the hero by means of her beauty and sex appeal. Otherwise, she is still mostly included to provide sexual interludes amidst the super-human feats of the macho man. Increasingly, the woman can survive as a model in advertisements as long as she maintains her size, shape and adheres to the style preferred by men. Companies sell their products by advertising the body image of the woman. Consequently, she is promoted from the status of a model to that of a heroine on the silver screen (obviously not by her histrionic talent) to flirt with the hero and make a large income. No doubt, women have a right to work, earn and at the same time be sexually liberated but it is unfortunate that she has to do it only to construct herself as desirable to men. In this process, they use their earning to buy the beauty as well as the body, represented by the media. Hence, both women's sexuality and earning power, which satisfy the liberated sensibilities of the female audience, are to a large extent, controlled by the common interests of patriarchy and capitalism, which are exploited by the media to the full.

Women are buying their gender identity but it is described in accordance with the masculinity at the heart of patriarchy and the corporate power of the beauty industry. Female stars/celebrities have added news value as elite personalities. But they too represent femininity as a whole, in the sense that they dominate news, special features, and TV programs and thus contribute to the popular images of women. The second type of women includes models and film stars who are young, skinny, fair and sexy and thus suit the standards set by men. The message is that to become a popular and rich star, women must have the kind of look which allures men. Hence, being sexy (and financial success are modeled on a certain body image. On the other hand, it is often seen that when these stars become obese and out of shape, they turn to soap operas, playing the roles of mother or villainous mothers - in- law. It is interesting to note that in most Indian soaps, the success or popularity of such characters depends on the shape of their body.

Generally, food and cooking are markers of femininity and they are deeply sensual and feminine only in the private domestic contexts of love and family. Most of the TV channels conduct cookery programs for the audience to take part in and win prizes. But in the public world of restaurant business, cooking is associated with professional men. This gender split is replicated in cookery programs on local channels where women are projected femininely in their domestic kitchens, while men occupy and supervise the busy business of 'restauranteering'. One of the producers of women's program on cookery remarked that it is wonderful to witness the spark of victory in the eyes of the winner when she receives her cheque. The reason is obvious – she is never rewarded for her cooking which is normally considered to be too routine a drudgery because in ninety percent of Indian homes cooking is still a woman's job. Hence, to reject it, is to reject femininity and all the other symbols of femininity such as motherhood, family, home et cetera. Films and television reinforce these associations with adult femininity (for the consumption of the audience) whereas frail, skinny, young and sexy femininity is the route to love and power of a different kind.

Western research shows that this kind of stereotyping of women by media significantly affects the minds of young women and if they are not thin and slender then it increases their dissatisfaction with their own identity and worth. The dominance of body aesthetics correlated with sex, success and money in the commercial world of film and advertising is affecting the way young girls think about their career in the world of fashion, beauty and fame. For example, in the South Indian film industry, mega heroes prefer tall, thin and slender teenage girls as their heroines to play the romantic intermission in their films. One of the studies of the Indian film Industry reveals that it is becoming increasingly difficult for film producers to get new faces/ bodies each time they make a film with these super heroes. Thus, the fascination for a slender female shape is getting established with the increase of female models that are young and skinny. But in real life, what percentage of women absorb these images and measure their femininity against them? Does the success of a film or soap opera depicting this kind of femininity indicate that it is acceptable to the female audience, especially in informed societies? It is obvious that only the mediated women set and follow these artificial standards. Constant exposure to media stereotyping lead the young girls to believe in these illusionary models and create false basis for judgments and actions.

Studies on TV/film-viewing audience show that glamorous body representations have greater impact on women spectators than on men.

Moreover, it is the nature (quality, context and type) of the films/programs, which is more significant in affecting the young women's minds towards a thin body image rather than the amount of exposure to these texts. The abundant focus on size and shape especially in the case of film heroines sideline other aspects of a woman's personality such as histrionics, facial expressions, adaptability and the like which are more important in terms of evaluation and comparison. In this whole scenario, what appears to be incontrovertible is that young college girls under the influence of the media, sometimes react more negatively towards themselves by following unscrupulous eating habits, while the adult women exhibit a more holistic sense of self-identity.

In urban middle class societies obsession with weight is increasingly growing in the young girls. Many slimming centers charging exorbitant prices have cropped up, alluring young and middle aged women. For example, in the advertisement of a successful urban slimming centre the girl says: "I have always been a socialite. My bubbly personality wooed every one but after the weight loss I can see not just appreciating eyes but also the shutter bugs focusing at me." (The Hindu, 7 June, 2007). As a result, this false image creates a propensity towards hyperactive body exercises, inadequate eating obsession et cetera. among the young girls. Hence the media representation of female body image is very narrow and one-sided and exploits weak and psychologically disturbed young girls. In short, these images are 'politically oppressive' and 'commercially exploitative'.

In fact, every woman is sensitive to the idea of weight reduction in a healthy way of course. Perhaps she tries to display her best looks and camouflage the negative aspects of her body i.e. the size and shape.

As Woodward states "women read the slender body and appropriate the messages they find there in different ways: those messages are enacted in the context of personal situation and personal history" (quoted by Wykes and Gunter: 143).

This kind of exaggerated and unrealistic representation of women's selves across a wide range of media is probably infuriating and frustrating to most urban women who perhaps hover in between the two positions (the ideal self and the real self) in the continuum of self value judgments. This false representation of femininity has a larger impact on vulnerable and uninformed spectators in the society in their understanding of how women are valued in the broader social context of socio-cultural values and roles. These ideas of femininity neither comply with the reality of women's experience nor are helpful in combating on going inequalities, abuses and atrocities on women which constitute the day-to-day experiences of women in their real lives.

Moreover, the mass media's representation of womanhood sets limits and controls on the woman's individuality and the value assigned to them, by imposing a false standard of what is and what is not desirable. This leads us to an important realization – that in reality, nothing has changed since the time of the second-wave feminism, other than perhaps what is indicated by legislation. In conclusion it seems that although women are competing with men, they are still over burdened by a 'sex saturated' culture in which almost everything is measured according to physical appearance. Probably how they survive this overriding assault is a challenge to the strength and willpower of a majority of women consumers of media texts across the world.

References

Brooker, Will and Jermyn, Deborah (ed.). *The Audience Studies Reader*. Routledge, London, New York (2003).

Gamble, Sarah. *The Routledge Companion to Feminism and Postfeminism*. UK: 2006. (first published in 1999).

Radway, Janice: *Reading the Romance: Women, Patriarchy and Popular Literature*, Chapel Hill: University of North Carolina Press, (1984). (taken from *The Audience Studies Reader*).

Rodman, George: *Making Sense of Media:An Introduction to Mass Communication*, Allyn & Bacon, Boston, London (2001).

Thornham, Sue (ed.). *Feminist Film Theory, A Reader*. Edinburgh University Press, Edinburgh (1999).

Wykes, Maggie and Gunter, Barrie: *The Media and Body Image*. Sage publications, London, New Delhi (2005).

6.

Two Faces of Women on Television: Need for a Gender Policy?

C. MRUNALINI

Women on television need to be discussed under two heads: women in media (as work force) and women as media subjects (as content in media). Another category is that of women as viewers. Women as viewers are also participants in a significant way. It has been established beyond doubt that all over the world, women constitute a considerable percentage of television viewers. In India, perhaps the percentage of female television viewers is even higher as television constitutes the chief source of entertainment for moderately educated middle-class women. A lot has been said about how badly women are portrayed in soap operas and how these serials, in all languages, are reinforcing the stereotypical female image. Much has also been said about the way women are portrayed in advertisements. Through this paper, I will try to build up an argument in favour of a *Gender Policy* in media.

Indian media, whether print or electronic, has recently been facing serious questions about the lack of a policy where women and depiction of women's issues are concerned. Print media has often been criticised for publishing advertisements which are demeaning to women, in the same pages where women's issues are seriously discussed. But such objections are rarely met with serious consideration by policy makers because media is, in the ultimate analysis, only a business enterprise. Advertisements give revenue which can obviously not be ignored by any policy maker. Conceding that advertisements, whether in print or television, are an unavoidable aspect of media, the question that can be asked is, why should there be such a difference in projecting gender issues in the news and the serials? In most channels, news and news-stories attempt to be gender sensitive, in fact, they even go overboard with slogans on women's welfare and women's empowerment. But, the same channels have serials in which male chauvinism is rampant. Which of these two faces of the channel is to be accepted as its ideological front? The same channel telecasts informed discussions on women's issues as well as soaps perpetrating stereotypical representations of women. While the former is limited to an afternoon telecast, the latter takes over prime slots. Again the question is: Is there some gender policy guiding a channel's vision?

It is in this context that, as a regular participant on television channels, I interacted with the following categories of women to elicit their response on television and its impact on women:

- The average common viewers, on whom the television serials have the greatest impact.
- Women producers.
- Women's organizations which have been fighting against gender bias that colour representations of women in media.

The following issues were discussed:

1. Representation of women in TV serials.
2. The effect of these images on women viewers.
3. The timing of women's programmes on channels: As they are nearly always during noon, it is assumed that women's programmes are meant only for home makers. Why is it assumed that men and working women need not see them?
4. The glaring gap in perspective on women's issues in the news stories and the popular serials.

The results of the feedback are quite revealing:

Women Viewers

1. Women who are in the age group of 60 and above, found the characters in serials disgusting and unreal. Women in the age group of 30 to 40 found them interesting and they confessed that these characters do impact their lives. For them these characters embody an element of

wish fulfillment. This is also the case with films but the difference is that while cinema is accepted as a make-believe world, TV serials are considered to be much closer to reality. In that sense, as most middle-age women conceded, television has a stronger impact. A study by Purnima Mankekar of Stanford University seems to have come up with such findings. I quote from a review of Mankekar's work:
"She demonstrates how television in India has profoundly shaped women's place in the family, community and nation and how it has played a crucial role in the realignment of class, caste, consumption, religion and politics."

2. My own findings are perfectly in agreement with this position. In one case, the impact was so much that one viewer confessed that she had to take psychiatric help to get back to normalcy. She had become asocial, started suspecting and disliking her loved ones and often felt depressed. It took her time and regular interaction with a psychiatrist to realize that her agony was a result of her identification with some characters of the daily soaps. She is now a happier person, having stopped watching those serials. This may be an extreme case, but is symptomatic of the kind of disturbance caused by some of the tele-serials.

3. The television authorities schedule socially relevant women's programmes, which show gender issues in an objective perspective, in such time slots when only home makers and retired people can watch them. At the same time, the soaps are almost always slotted for prime time. When they are repeatedly questioned about this, they say that they can't afford to schedule them in prime time, because there are no 'takers' for it (implying ad revenue). But, it is not commercial reasons alone that influence this decision. It is the policy itself which believes that gender sensitive programmes are only an 'unavoidable burden' to be carried for the sake of political correctness and hence can only claim 'token' honour. When a channel accepts that these shows are only for tokenism, there is nothing much left to be said since most reformist gestures are often nothing but gestures of tokenism. But, when a channel projects itself as gender-sensitive and committed to gender justice, such tokenism falls short of all expectations.

Women Producers

Many of the producers of television serials are women, to name a few–Ekta Kapoor, Aruna Irani, Deepti Bhatnagar and Radhika Sarath Kumar. In fact, Hindi television soaps seem to be dominated by one single woman–Ekta Kapoor. The real question though, is the mindset of the producer and not the gender of the producer. Madhavi Mutatkar, president Zee TV, believes, "If a *saas-bahu* tear-jerker is successful on one channel there is immediate commercial pressure to put another on air. In many ways, these serials have brought real empowerment to women. A housewife sitting with the remote in her hand is the queen of all she surveys with FMCG companies and the white goods industries vying for her attention."

Whether holding the remote denotes 'empowerment' is better left to a thinking person's discretion.

Another claim by the producers (male or female) is that they show women managing large business, i.e. women who are empowered and competitive. But, how do these on-screen so called empowered women behave? They are often driven by motives of revenge and envy and professional women on screen are often depicted as negative characters. They dress provocatively, they use gestures of domination and guile, their language is violent and they certainly offer no role model for emulation. This image is no better or for that matter much worse than the other stereotype of women as being submissive, tolerant, suffering and sacrificing souls. This distorted representation of women professionals is indeed extremely detrimental to the cause of empowerment.

Role of Women Activists

The women's organizations came out with two suggestions:

- Demand a regulatory body for television serials, on the lines of the Censor Board. This should be constituted after holding meetings all over the state and gathering consensus from women from all walks of life.

Start an alternative channel. This is a very tempting idea, but is there necessary capital for it? Is it sustainable?

What seems to go against all that women activism is trying to achieve, is the promotion of cinema on television. No TV channel can survive without movie-based programs. They are indeed the mainstay of television. The way films and audience-based shows are projected on television, is indeed appalling. Recently a leading TV news channel gave tremendous mileage to a film called *Rakhee*, where the brother of the heroine indulges in large scale homicide to end dowry. He kills all men who demand dowry in the most gruesome manner, because his sister had died a dowry-death. The film was hailed as a feminist film, the director the only feminist director in Telugu films, so on and so forth. This channel called women viewers to meet the director and some of these women became emotionally overwhelmed and said: "how we wish we had a brother like NTR to protect us or take revenge on our behalf?". The whole effort of women's movement to make women self-reliant, self-sufficient and empowered enough to fight their own battles is simply defeated by such films which are upheld as feminist films. The female characters in the film, including the girl who sings around the trees with the hero, do nothing for the cause. They are not participants in this movement against dowry. The protagonist does not inspire a single man or woman to emulate him, which, at least would have given the story greater validity and claim. Perhaps the TV shows on such films have more effect than the films themselves, because they influence the perceptions of the viewers.

According to one study, TV viewing increases the risk of violence by five times. So much for the claims of TV Producers that television is only a make-believe world like cinema and has no impact on its audience. So much for the claims of women producers who think they are creating self-reliant business women in their serials and serving the cause of women's empowerment.

The Final Question

TV channels which telecast these tear-jerking serials also put up discussions on current issues which concern women and are by women, thereby attempting an awareness arousing exercise. But the question is:

Which of the two images, the one of women as seen in serials or those of women as participants in the issue-based discussions, is the image that the television channel wants to project?

This is a question women viewers might also like to ask. All TV channels have discussion forums which represent contemporary thought on women's issues. The same channels churn out serials of age-old regressive values and norms, which are extremely judgmental about women. In the absence of some policy on gender matters, a couple of discussion programs are not going to make any difference to the general damage being done by television to the social movement for gender justice, which has begun to gain ground in India only recently. Has the time not come for women to demand a Gender Policy from Television Barons?

Having been part of television programming for 20 odd years I had occasion to question the decision-makers in the field. Why can't they have a policy regarding gender? They have policies on politics, individuals, language, education but not gender. Where gender is concerned, the issues are viewed only as segments. The viewers of *Naree-Bheri* (a serious discussion forum for women on ETV 2, aired every Sunday) are seen as different from the innumerable viewers that watch serials on the sister channel (ETV) day in and day out. Gender issues are not what they would count for their credibility. Where gender is concerned it seems safer and more beneficial to hold on to adhocism. Besides, all gender-justice talk is confined to forum discussions and is considered to make no difference to the everyday lives of women. It is important that television viewers, producers, program makers, media watchers and women activists together press for some clarity in matters relating to the understanding of women's issues and demand that a gender policy be evolved for the creation of a more socially responsible media.

PART II

Framing Women

7.

Images of Women in Indian Soap Operas

WAHEEDA SULTANA

A soap opera is an ongoing, episodic work of fiction/non fiction usually broadcast on television or radio and more recently on mobile phones. Indian soap operas (written, filmed, enacted and produced mostly by Indians for an Indian audience), with episodes broadcast on a daily/weekly/semi-weekly basis on Indian television channels/channel chains (Star Network, Sony Entertainment, Sun Network, Doordarshan) are not always limited to India alone, but are broadcast overseas in the UK, USA, and some parts of Europe, South Africa, and Australia.

The term 'soap opera' was coined by the American press in the 1930s to denote the extraordinarily popular genre of serialized domestic radio dramas, which by 1940, represented some 90 per cent of all commercially-sponsored daytime broadcast hours. The 'soap' in soap opera alluded to their sponsorship by soap manufacturers while 'opera' suggested an ironic incongruity between the domestic narrative concerns of the daytime serial and the most elevated of dramatic forms.

The defining quality of the soap opera form is its seriality. A serial narrative is a story told through a series of individual, narratively linked installments. Unlike episodic television programs in which there is no narrative linkage between episodes and each episode tells a more or less self-contained story, the viewer's understanding of and pleasure in any given serial installment is predicated, to some degree, upon his or her knowledge of what has happened in previous episodes. Furthermore, each serial episode always leaves the narrative with loose ends for the next episode to take up. The viewer's relationship with serial characters is also different from those in episodic television. In the latter, characters cannot undergo changes that transcend any given episode, and they seldom reference events from previous episodes. Serial characters do change across episodes (they age and even die), and they possess both histories and memories. Television serials are not merely narratively segmented; its episodes are designed to be parceled out in regular installments, so that both the telling of the serial story and its reception by viewers is institutionally regulated.

Soaps are principally sources of entertainment, providing pleasure and enjoyment, though they also aim to provide considerable food for thought as the viewers mull over the problems that are thrown to them. Contemporary soaps employ a number of standard conventions. According to Sonia Livingstone, the common soap opera features include

> Transmission of regular, frequent times, often daily; predominantly aimed at female viewers, occupying day-time/early evening slots; use of fairly constant and large cast, over many years, and a faithful audience; cheap production costs, regarded as low prestige entertainment; concern with daily activities, centered on a small community and/or large family; simulation of real time and realistic events; interwoven narratives, with overlapping resolutions; 'cliff-hangers' to ensure committed viewing; focus on female characters and 'feminine' or domestic concerns.

Films and film-based shows dominated Indian television programming schedules in its early years. As television producers and channels matured, the focus changed: serials, sitcoms and soaps became more successful. Today, there is no dearth of soap operas for viewers on Indian television channels. At least one third of India's billion inhabitants regularly watch Indian soap operas, which have displaced popular cinema as the prime entertainment genre. Further, among the Indian diaspora on every continent, Indian soap operas are a feature of life, a source of pleasure, discussion and shared identity.

Manohar Shyam Joshi is considered 'The Father of Indian Soap Operas'. His first social content soap opera, *Hum Log* (We People) was telecast on July, 1984 on Doordarshan. The obvious objectives of this program were the promotion of family planning and elevation of the status of women, and the main characters and their interactions catered to the realization of these objectives. One important point to be noted about this early attempt at the making of an Indian soap opera is its strong social commitment. This serial inaugurated family dramas on television, and family, as an important social and cultural value, was forged here. The Indian public loved the show, the characters became legends and touched the hearts of the Indian audience. Joshi's other memorable creations include *Buniyad Kakaji Kahin*, *Mungeri Lal ke Haseen Sapne*, *Humrahi*, *Zameen Aasman* and *Gatha*.

The Indian Soap opera which began with *Hum Log* continued to address social issues, particularly those related to women in a family. The creation of women of substance who upheld values both in and outside the family has been one of the dominant features of some of the successful soaps in the 80s and early 90s. For instance, popular film and television actress, Priya Tendulkar, shot into limelight in the 1980s by playing the lead role in a popular television serial, *Rajni*. Rajni is an average home maker who demands fair play in everything—everything she buys and every service she pays for. This character made the entire nation consumer conscious, which was no mean achievement. She was a busybody who took on everyone, and the audience loved it. A responsible, bold and assertive homemaker who fights for her rights in every aspect of life was seen as an asset to the family as well as society. On the positive side, Rajni's character enhanced the dignity of a home maker; on the negative side it re-forged home as the arena for a woman's assertion and realization, taking the risk of emphasizing the stereotype that a woman's place is at home. However, on the whole, Rajni was a woman with whom millions of Indian women could relate to and her fight for justice was certainly inspiring.

One of the earliest serials to showcase women's empowerment and project women as successful professionals was *Udaan* (1990). It portrayed the real-life story of Kanchan Choudhary who was later appointed as the first Director General of Police in Uttaranchal. The story of the struggle of a young woman from an ordinary family, to become an IPS officer, did offer a positive role model for young viewers. That it was not fiction but a real life story of someone in the immediate world, added to the credibility of the story and the popularity of its protagonist. *Humraahi* produced by Roger Pereira, went on air in January 1992, again on Doordarshan. It dealt with the status of women, addressing issues such as the age of marriage, age of first pregnancy, gender bias in childbearing and child rearing, equal educational opportunities for boys and girls, and free choice in marriage for women.

A clear and significant shift in the representation of women in Indian soap operas occurred towards the end of the last decade of the twentieth century with what are popularly known as '*Saas-Bahu*' serials obtaining unprecedented viewer ratings and climbing high on the popularity scale. Here again, family is at the centre of the story; often it is a large Hindu joint family with a responsible daughter-in-law, who is dedicated to the welfare of the family, and steers the family out of a variety of tribulations including family feuds, business losses, financial crises, besides other unavoidable situations triggered by fate to reverse the family's fortunes. Some of the most popular examples of this sub-genre of Indian soaps are: *Kyunki Saas Bhi Kabhi Bahu Thi, Kahani Ghar Ghar Ki, Kasauti Zindagi ki, Desh Mein Nikla Hoga Chand, Kumkum, Bhabhi.* The central characters in these soaps re-forge the stereotype of a traditional Hindu daughter-in-law dressed in saris wearing sindur, and mangalsutra. The wicked and villainous women are often more fashionably dressed, often wearing more modern, western outfits. These contrasts become significant since they imply value judgements, linking the women's attire to their attitude.

Women as Viewers

Several women watch soaps, perhaps due to the romantic attraction that these soaps have. Some women are attracted to soaps because, in certain ways, the soaps seem to mirror their day-to-day existence. Through their association with soaps, these women construct pleasures and meanings for themselves. The progress of soaps becomes a topic of conversation when women get together. The characters of the serials become more or less like family members for many of the viewers. Viewers discuss the lives of characters from these soaps–'Tulsi', 'Prerna', 'Parvati', 'Saloni'– as if they are their acquaintances or relatives. The soaps often become a topic of discussion at the workplace for some women. To keep the family drama interesting, soap makers put into the story all the ingredients that they imagine are of interest for women: huge and affluent homes, rich costumes and jewelry, romance and gossip, extra-marital relations and illegitimate children, among other societal scandals. The vexing question as to whether the soap makers churn out such stuff because women really like them or women consume the stuff simply because this is all that is churned out can never be decisively answered, but the damage done by the representations of women in these soaps is too large to be ignored.

More recently a new trend appears to be emerging – that of showcasing the contemporary woman as one who achieves her goals in life by grit and not by manipulation. Unfortunately, this positive reflection of women is evident in only a few soaps such as *Jassi Jaissi Koi Nahin, Koi Dil Mein Hain, Saaksshi, Kuch Kehna Hai Mujhko Yeh Meri Life Hai* and *Saath Phere*. These soaps are based on the central theme that a woman's life is not only about beauty, husband and kids and that aspirations, creativity and financial independence are not just a man's prerogative. The serial *Jassi Jaisi Koi Nahin* has broken the myth that good looks are necessary for the post of a personal secretary. Jassi embodies a the struggle of a modern Indian woman. *Jassi* has been such a great success among the viewers that a recent advertisement for a secretary states "We want Jassi too". The serial did indeed go a long way in instilling confidence in average looking girls. For the first time, the Indian Postal Services Department has issued a stamp on a fictitious character, Jassi. This young woman was chosen for this rare honour because, her grit, knowledge and hard work seemed to convey a positive message. *Saath Phere–Yehi hai Saloni ka Safar*, is the story of Saloni, a dark complexioned 24-year old girl. Her talent is overshadowed by her complexion. Faced with such a situation, Saloni refuses to give in to societal pressures and prejudices and embarks upon a journey to search for her own unique identity. Serials of this kind, no doubt raise an important issue concerning women: how in the case of a woman, beauty and complexion become an important criteria for success.

There are a variety of women characters representing several stereotypes, in these shows. This perhaps makes it more interesting for women to watch, especially if they can relate to one or the other kind of woman projected on the screen. Most strikingly, soap operas contain a very large number of characters, and this provides the audience with diverse points of view with which to identify. Soap opera, like any other form of drama, requires both elements of good and bad. If there are only good or only bad characters the viewers get bored. Both elements need to be combined. In these serials for every single, strong woman, there are scores of evil and fraudulent women whose intrigue, ill-will, jealousy and villainy indeed become necessary components to establish the power and virtue of the heroine. Many women are projected in the various Indian television soaps as schemers, plotters and vamps. The audience is given no choice but to hate these characters that depict the face of evil. These evil women are charged with a huge share of what are traditionally branded female vices in a patriarchal world, such as envy, jealousy, dishonesty, gossip, tale-telling besides more dangerous ones such as vengefulness and seduction. For example Sudha Chandran as Romola Sikand, the manipulative villain in

Kahin Kissii Roz , Shweta Kawatra as Esha, the trouble maker in *Kusum*; Urvashi Dholakia as Komolika in *Kasautii Zindagii Kay*, Rakhee Tandon as Ruby, the other woman in *Heena* have indeed popularly become known on Indian television as women who embody female villainy.

The creation of strong, believable characters seems to be essential for the appeal of any soap. These strong women like Tulsi, Prerna, Kusum, Parvati and others are everything the viewers admire. The viewers want to do the kind of things their favourite characters do, both in their public as well as private life. Many TV characters like Tulsi, Kusum, Heena, Parvati, Jassi, Prerna and others have become household names. Most of the TV actors are perhaps better-known than many film stars who make news one Friday and disappear the next. Sumita Hattangadi of the market research agency 'Third Eye' explains the strong and widespread identification with Tulsi and Parvati: "These are seen as achievable role models unlike famous real people such as Kiran Bedi and Indira Gandhi. Ordinary women find a resonance of their own problems and concerns in these serials. Some ape the characters and adopt their dress sense and even start wearing bindis worn by the soap opera characters."

Women as Producers of Soap Operas

Women participate in television programming on three levels – as viewers, as actresses/anchors and as makers of the programmes. As actresses and viewers, women constitute a sizeable majority, though their numbers are still few and far between at the production level. Some of the popular serial producers include Ekta Kapoor, Aruna Irani, Deepti Bhatnagar and Vinita Nanda. Of these, Ekta Kapoor has the largest number of titles to her credit and she is the successful propagator of the *Saas-Bahu* type serials. Ekta Kapoor, dubbed as the queen of Indian soap operas, took to production at the age of 19. Daughter of Jeetendra, a well known film actor, she is the creative head of Balaji Telefilms. This unit incorporated in 1994 is a family run TV Production Company based in Mumbai and. She has created more than 20 soaps on major Indian networks, and a comedy series *Hum Panch* (We Five). Her popular serials such as *Kahani Ghar Ghar Ki, Kyunki Saas Bhi Kabhi Thi, Kasuti Zindagi Kay, Kahin To Hoga, Kutumb* and others are spread across a number of channels such as Star Plus, Zee, Sony and Sun Network. Most of her serials revolve around one theme – a woman who copes with humanly insurmountable difficulties to save the honour and wealth of her huge joint family. The formula developed by Ekta Kapoor has been phenomenally successful on the Indian television and is being doled out in lethal measures. Aruna Irani, one time famous Hindi film star is now into producing TV soaps. Her *Mehandi Tere Naam ki* is based on Indian immigrant life in London and mainly revolves round a stereotypical love triangle motif. Not much is changed by the fact that it is a woman who is steering the show. Deepti Bhatnagar, formerly a well-known model too has taken to production of TV serials. She produced some very interesting travel related serials, *Musafir Hoon Yaaron* and *Yatra*. In these shows however, the focus is not on portrayal of women's issues. Vinita Nanda, associated with the satellite TV right from its inception, worked as an assistant director with Raman Kumar for some of the successful soaps of the 90's – *Tara* and *Yeh Jo hai Jindagi*. She then co-produced *Guniram* with Raman Kumar. *Guniram* is the story of a villager who comes to the city and makes mistakes which only makes him more loveable. Her *Puraskar* is about children who have won bravery awards. It was *Tara*, for which she wrote the script, which catapulted her into fame. Vinita Nanda's interests are varied: she runs an NGO called 'Project Smita Society', makes documentaries, and writes for films besides writing and producing serials. Her work is marked by a serious societal concern. Her themes range from the impact of terrorism on women to dowry travails faced by young brides. More such writers and producers will indeed make a difference to the promotion of gender justice on the small screen.

If we take an objective estimate of the number of women involved in making television shows, we will find that it is still dismally low. Under-represented, both in front of and behind the scenes, women still struggle to cross the gender gap in the entertainment and news industry. Unless more and more creative women with critical thinking abilities begin to take to TV production, the scenario of female representation on the small screen will not change for the better. With the laws of globalization controlling all industries, and more particularly the media, only large production houses with huge investments are able to dominate the media space and therefore decide the nature of the media culture. This makes any form of innovation difficult. In soap operas we have a very powerful medium which can bring about transformations in existing gender perceptions, and a qualitative difference in looking at women, their experiences, lives and problems; but this potential is yet to be fully exploited.

References

Bell, Phillip and Hanet, Kari. "Film, TV and the Popular". *The Australian Journal of media and Culture*, Vol.1 No.2 (1987).

Burell, Patrica M. "Women & Soap Operas: A Cultural Perspective", *Social Science Journal,* Vol. 37 No.1 (2000).

Das, K Tridwip. "The New Women on Telly", *Femina*, June, 2004.

Abercrombie, Nicholas, *Television and Society*. Cambridge: Polity Press,1996.

Buckingham, D. *Public Secrets: 'EastEnders' and its Audience*. London: BFI,1987.

Geraghty, C. *Women and Soap Opera*. Cambridge: Polity Press,1991.

Kilborn, R. *Television Soaps*, London: Batsford,1992.

Livingstone, S. *Making Sense of Television*. Oxford: Pergamon, 1990.

McQuail, D. *Mass Communication Theory*. London: Sage, 1987.

Morley, D. *Family Television*. London: Routledge (The Routledge edition was published in 1988).

Talwar, Shyaonti. *The TV Stranglehold in India, www.rediff.com* (7 January 2003).

Venkatraman, Latha. "Back on her Feet and in Action". *Financial Daily* (19, April 2004).

8.
"People Said I Created Pornography": Sexuality, the Gaze and Rituparno Ghosh

SOMDATTA MANDAL

From the very beginning of his career, since he made *Unishe April* (1995), acclaimed Bengali filmmaker Rituparno Ghosh has made films with women protagonists, so much so that he has often been labelled "the woman's director of Bangla (Bengali) cinema." His explanation for his oeuvre is simple – he merely feels that he understands the inner feelings of women, their passion, agony and suffering. All his films up to *Titli* (2001) dealt with women-centric situations, they are either about the new woman, the lonely woman, the rebellious woman or the persecuted woman. Ever since he adapted Tagore's *Chokher Bali* (*Sand in the Eye*, 2003) and Tarashankar Bandyopadhyay's short story "Protima" as *Antarmahal* (*Views of the Inner Chamber*, 2005), Rituparno has been mired in controversy for making films with too much, and often unnecessary, focus on sexuality and what film critics like Laura Mulvey call 'visual pleasure' and 'the gaze'. In Rituparno's case the situation is further complicated by three factors – his own preference for alternative sexuality, his constant harping on the statement, "I feel I understand the inner feelings of women, their passion, agony and suffering" (Mandal: 18), and his own declaration about the androgynous nature of human characters: "I believe in the art of androgyny which includes the male and female opinion."

Through a detailed discussion of *Chokher Bali* and *Antarmahal*, I will focus upon some of these issues and try to analyze why the director feels that he understands the psyche of women better, and hence can offer a more objective approach. It is also interesting to see how moving backwards in time and setting these two films in the nineteenth century, Rituparno bravely depicts relationships and sexual escapades of characters than he did in films set in contemporary times. Also the gender-sensitized director seems to have become more keen on cashing in on the global culture market's penchant for 'authentic' India (or Bengal), which can be constructed by invoking the past as it exists in the popular imagination. Thus we have ample bare-bodied women in the *zenana* (inner chamber) – young widows and mature first wives whose menstruating situations – described by the director in graphic details in both the films under discussion – point out to the viewers the latent sexual potentiality of suppressed womanhood.

Sexuality

Let us first take the example of *Chokher Bali*, a film subtitled 'A Passion Play'. Though the phrase encapsulates the complex web of desire into which the novel's two male and two female protagonists are inextricably caught, the person singled out for exclusive attention is Binodini. Ghosh transforms Rabindranath Tagore's avowedly psychological novel of triangular love into a period piece with his own version of the nation and its women. The deprivations, both sexual and material, that mark the life of an unusually gifted, educated, strong-willed and passionate young widow of Tagore's time, who willfully transgressed the code of conduct proper for her, provides the director with the convenient apparatus to showcase the apparently deglamourised sex appeal of Bollywood's diva Aishwarya Rai, cast in the role of Binodini. Anticipating opposition towards his film and creating a rationale for his departure from the original, Ghosh begins the film with a quote from Tagore in which the latter expresses regret about the ending of the novel: "Ever since *Chokher Bali* was published, I have always regretted the ending. I ought to be censured for it." (translation my own) In the original version, after a great tumult of adulterous passion between the widowed Binodini and Mahendra which precipitates a crisis threatening the latter's marriage, the novel concludes with a reconciliation of the married couple at the bedside of Rajlakshmi, Mahendra's dying mother. Binodini forgives both men and goes off to Benaras to lead the life of an ascetic. Ghosh is unwilling to accept this analysis. "Suddenly she becomes very clinical and antiseptic, devoid of all passion, because that is the right thing for a widow to do," says Ghosh in an interview with Asia Source.

> Tagore started this serialized novel with the forbidden passion of a widow, more because of reasons of titillation; he had to draw people to read his novel because he was editing the magazine! It got a bit out of hand midway, and all the holy Brahmins, their hair went up in holy smoke [laughs] and they almost started lambasting Tagore, so he himself not being a Hindu decided not to fiddle too much with Hindu sentiments and restored her to the conformist, Hindu domesticity that society demanded at that time.

In Ghosh's Barthesian reworking of the novel, there is no neat closure of the intense, claustrophobic, web of desires and jealousies set up between the protagonists. Instead, the ending is made much more complex, enigmatic and open in which the audience learns of Binodini's decision, through her letter written to Ashalata, to search for her 'desh' and simply going away to Kashi to live as a good Hindu widow. This 'desh' is not 'country' nor should it be translated or read as country, says Ghosh. It should be understood as a space, a domain for the independent woman that Binodini was. In another interview given to film critic Shoma A. Chatterjee in 2003, Rituparno commented on what inspired him to make a film on *Chokher Bali*:

> It was the delicate interplay of relationships that touched me. The story offered a vast matrix of relationships, which I, as director, could play around with in a myriad different ways. *Chokher Bali* struck me as a very original text to begin with. It deals with unfaithfulness in the man-woman relationship within the institution of marriage. Maybe, if you pick on this lack of faith, you may find that one common link between *Chokher Bali* and *Bariwali*. The 'period' flavour I could invest the film with was another attraction. Tagore's original story did not have any time reference. The characters seem to be hanging in a limbo. The film offered me the chance of preparing the 'period' for the film. In *Shatranj Ke Khilari*, Ray created the historical context for the film turning the 'period' into a 'character.' He did the same for *Ghare Baire* and *Charulata*. I have done the same in this film (Chatterjee: 223–24).

However, throughout the movie, Ghosh who has highlighted his research into making the film an authentic 'period' piece particularly in terms of setting, apparel and jewellery, has taken recourse to several incongruities regarding social norms of behaviour and codes of conduct that guided heterosexual interactions. Instances of physical intimacy of the married couple in their private chambers have been overdone no doubt, but in public (especially in the picnic scene where Ashalata and Mahendra lie huddled together) or Behari's entry into the puja room with a stranger asking for Binodini's signature for a campaign are held up as signs of such ahistorical approach. What is interesting to note is that the film's violation of historical and textual fidelity is closely linked to issues of sexuality. Critics point out that Binodini and Mahendra's dalliance in the *thakurghar* (room for prayer) is not only blasphemous but also historically inaccurate. Mahendra comes with the jewel box and touches her in an endearing way and although Binodini asks him to take her to the River Ganges, she clearly states that she does not want to take 'the middle path'. She wants Mahendra to accept their relationship in public, which obviously he cannot do. Mahendra calls her his '*pran bhomra*' (literally and metaphorically meaning the wasp that carries his life and soul) and when he kisses Binodini, she states, "My husband died of TB" and laughs at the shirking attitude of Mahendra, the would-be doctor. Other critics also note that although the novel does not allude to a consummation of the illicit relation between Mahendra and Binodini, the film flamboyantly displays their love and has several scenes of love-making, the most notable of which takes place inside a horse-drawn carriage where the passion of the lovers is offset by the sounds and sights of the rallies protesting British domination. What is disturbing is that Ghosh, in his attempt to visually translate the passion that informs the novel but remains unstated, resorts to hackneyed codes of representation of sexual passion reminiscent of twentieth century Hollywood. Later when Binodini sheds all her inhibitions, comes decked in gold ornaments to Behari asking him to marry her, she says, "You don't have to love me...take me." Though her proposal is rejected, she tries all the sexual mores possible to attract Behari's attention and rejects the attributes she is supposed to possess as a young woman and as a widow.

The urge to display overt sexuality gains even greater momentum in Ghosh's next film. Set in the late nineteenth century, 1878 to be exact, *Antarmahal* (*Views of the Inner Chamber*) is a definite period piece, bringing into focus the patriarchal *zamindari* system of rural Bengal with landlords keeping their wives hidden in the *zenana*. It is a brilliant depiction of the oppression women who suffered at the hands of their 'masters' – the *zamindars*, husbands and priests.

Bhubaneswar Chowdhury is a wealthy and tyrannical *zamindar* who has two obsessions: the first is his desperate attempt for an heir which even his new and young second wife Jashomati seems unable to deliver; and the second is to compete with his regional rivals to produce the most magnificent effigy for the annual Durga puja ceremony. He thus concocts a master plan of changing the face of the goddess to that of the most powerful woman on earth – Queen Victoria. This, he is sure, would fetch him the enviable title of 'Roy Bahadur'. Meanwhile his two wives, Mahamaya and Jashomati, try to look out for one another especially as Bhubaneswar begins to sexually assault his younger wife every night. He even brings a Brahmin priest to chant holy *shlokas* pleading to the gods of procreation (10th episode from Kalidasa's *Raghuvansha*) during the intercourse so that the brave exploits of mythological heroes would expedite the conception of a male heir. Traumatized and lonely, Jashomati is dangerously drawn to the young sculptor Braj Bushan who has been employed to create the new effigy of Durga. Despite the purdah system, Ghosh manages to create several situations in the film where the young Jashomati comes physically close to Braj Bhushan. The contrast between love and sex, male oppression and tender ministration is brought into the frame with teasing sensitivity. By the time the *zamindar* realizes that the face of the Goddess Durga has been modeled on his young wife and marches with his gun to shoot her, the woman has already committed suicide. The British painter who serves as the objective narrator of the story concludes the film with the following statement. "She died of an incurable malady. No one knows what happened to the young sculptor."

As a self-proclaimed expert in portraying relationships, in this film too Ghosh excels in developing the subtle nuances between characters, especially the interplay and interdependence of the two oppressed women, who are ironically juxtaposed against patriarchal adoration for supernatural heroines. But *Antarmahal* created quite a furore for Ghosh's blatant presentation of sex. Though some critics accused him of presenting pornography, Rituparno was quite nonchalant about the whole affair. In an interview given to Indrani Roy Mitra for the website rediff.com (November 22, 2005), he said that he failed to understand why Indians couldn't accept sexuality as a part of life. He expressed his sadness at the fact that the accusation of creating pornography came from a country that adores the architectural excellence of Khajuraho and takes pride in the *Kama Sutra*. He said:

> A film is but a mirror of life and so is *Antarmahal*. It spoke of the life and times as they were in nineteenth century Bengal. The period witnessed sexual exploitation and my job was to recreate it. Pornography is something that makes use of sex and sexuality to generate physical excitement. It's a pity that people are equating *Antarmahal* with cheap exhibitionism. The intimate scenes were not meant to entertain. They were meant to stir the audience's minds. The *zamindar* makes it a point to have sex with his wife every night so she can bear him a child. Their sexual interaction is a dry, mechanical process bereft of love and emotion. The wife is used and abused every night by her mindless husband. Through the oft-repeated 'intimate' scenes, my intent was not to focus on the sex but on the way the woman in question was exploited by her husband. People in our country are used to sexual overtones in literature, but not in films. I wish they would get rid of such inhibitions.

The director hoped that this kind of self-declared mission of exposing patriarchal oppression would lift the film from the accusations it has been facing since its release. Dubbed as 'Rituparno's porno', questions were raised whether the director could not have shown some of the intimate scenes more suggestively as did Satyajit Ray from whom he borrowed many tropes, ideas and scenes in both *Chokher Bali* and *Antarmahal*. For instance, the character of Jashomati, enacted by Soha Ali Khan seems to resemble the child-bride in Satyajit Ray's *Devi* (*The Goddess*, 1960) portrayed by her mother Sharmila Tagore. Ray was too much of a puritan to project sex in anything but in silhouette and could never imagine going into the graphic scenes of sexual subjugation. Justifying these scenes Rituparno further states:

> The crux of the matter is that people have become so used to seeing middle class ethos and life patterns in my films, that they just cannot accept *Antarmahal* which is a conscious deviation from the known path. They are more irked as the film appears to be laden with sexual overtones. Why can't they understand that it is meant for adults, for whom sex is an indispensable part of life?

He even mentions that in keeping with the fidelity of the story, he wanted to depict the younger wife running out nude in the open courtyard, but could not do so fearing the censor scissors.

The Gaze

Film critics and feminists have discussed the meaning and possibilities of the 'gaze' over and over again. Before delving into analyzing how Rituparno uses the 'gaze' as a trope in both these movies, I would like to discuss a little about the theoretical issues related to the prevalence of the male gaze across cultures, something that Bell Hooks describes as Hollywood's patriarchal cinematic practice of "explicitly representing the woman as an object of a phallocentric gaze." The concept of the 'gaze' as distinct from that of the 'look' requires attention here, and we can use 'look' to connote a process, a relation, while using the word 'gaze' for a one-way subjective vision. The 'gaze' came into film theory, as most people know, through Laura Mulvey's influential 1975 essay, "Visual Pleasure and Narrative Cinema." In that essay, Mulvey alternated between using 'gaze' and 'look' for the phenomena she was describing. In the section titled "Woman as Image, Man as Bearer of the Look," Mulvey almost immediately replaces 'look' with 'gaze' when she says that "The determining male gaze projects its fantasy on to the female figure which is styled accordingly" (Mulvey: 11). She proceeds to show how "an active-passive heterosexual division of labour has ...controlled narrative structure," and to discuss differences between scopophilic and narcissistic pleasure in looking. Although in one section Mulvey talks about "the gaze of the spectator and that of the male characters in the film," and notes that "man is reluctant to gaze at his exhibitionist like," when she summarizes her points at the end she returns to the word 'look.' She distinguishes three cinematic 'looks': that of the camera in the pro-filmic event; that of the spectators in the cinema; and a third look that denies the first two and subordinates them to it, namely, that of the characters towards one another "within the screen illusion"(Mulvey: 17). Mulvey does not appear to see any difference between the 'look' and the 'gaze'. As a one-way subjective vision, the 'gaze' is distinguished from 'look' as a strategy for opening up space for process in looking, and E. Ann Kaplan emphasizes that the difference between the two words is significant and should be considered seriously.

It is true that 'gaze' reduces the 'woman/man' to a mere 'body.' In the highly and historically patriarchal Bengali society, looking connotes curiosity about 'The Other', a desire to know (which can of course be oppressive but does not have to be), while the gaze involves extreme anxiety – an attempt, in a sense, not to know, (but) to deny. Rituparno Ghosh amply uses all the three types of gazes in the films under discussion. In *Chokher Bali* he uses the sartorial codes of early nineteenth century Bengali women, which did not include any upper body garment, to allow the camera to rest on the exposed shoulder and back of Ashalata and Binodini. As Chakrabarti and Ganguly rightly point out, perhaps the most memorable excess of this fetish is displayed in the scene in which the modern (read western) educated Binodini teaches Ashalata how to wear a blouse/jacket (257). It appears that Ghosh cannot resist quoting Satyajit Ray of *Ghare Baire* (The Home and the World, 1984) where he uses a long sequence of Bimala trying on her new jackets. For Satyajit Ray, the woman's jacket becomes a metonym for the emerging *bhadramohila* (the new bourgeois gentlewoman) in the context of western modernity. However, for Ghosh this is an opportunity to titillate the audience. Aishwarya Rai, the heroine of *Chokher Bali* might not fit the description of Tagore's Binodini as a woman with smouldering sexuality who has "joined eyebrows, sharp glance, flawless features and a voluptuous youthfulness", however she still tries to trail the end of her white sari on the floor with her waist-length hair seldom tied. Her box-office glamour prevents the audience to think of her as a woman with earthy sexuality and unfulfilled passion.

But apart from the gaze of the spectator and that of the male characters in the film looking upon the woman's body as subject/object, in Rituparno's films the situation is often reversed too. Rituparno's feminist focus entails an interest in subjectivity, interiority, and relatedness – all of them approached through psychoanalysis. Reminiscent of the protagonist in Ray's film *Charulata* (*The Lonely Wife*, 1964), in *Chokher Bali*, when Binodini looks at distant objects through the opera glasses her vision pans the ghats of Benaras but focuses primarily on the wrestlers exercising. In the scene where they go for a picnic, Behari volunteers to get down into the pond to pick up some lotus. Through Binodini's eyes, the camera focuses on the bare-bodied, figure of Behari – something which according to some critics seems like "a stereotypical, MTV endorsed western gaze, which commodifies the male body" (Chakravarti & Ganguly: 256). At the same time, they argue that this post-modern gaze obliterates the subtle but powerful suggestion of homo-social bonding between Behari and Mahendra that informs the novel.

In *Antarmahal*, the elder wife Mahamaya, shocked to see the bare body of the young artisan, gets a screen fixed on the verandah in an attempt to prevent the younger wife Jashomoti from exposing herself to him, while she feeds the birds. Yet we cannot forget her own look of erotic longing as the Bihari sculptor shivers in his sleep in the outer courtyard. She also has a screen erected in the bedroom between the mantra-chanting Brahmin and the couple. Using the age-old trope of female seduction, Mahamaya tries to distract the priest's attention but inevitably leads herself to become a commodity for sexual enjoyment for the Brahmins. But coming back to the subject of female gaze, there are several scenes in the film where she looks out of the window rather voyeuristically at the young sculptor bathing in the pond, as is the more overt one when she sees the bare body and legs of the man for the first time and throws down a dhoti for him to cover himself up. Rituparno can be thus applauded in bringing into focus the idea of female desire through the female gaze, a subject hardly projected in commercial films. On the other hand, he has also been criticized for exploiting the sexual fantasies of the young sculptor. He has faced severe criticism from the sculptor community for suggestive scenes and for attempts to titillate the viewer's sexual desires. Though taking liberties with the original plot of the story, Ghosh's good intention of portraying the various tales of oppression, of aged husbands raping wives half their age, of society making fun of wives unable to bear children, of priests taking advantage of helpless housewives and so on is quite successful. He also does well by lending a subtle treatment to the romance that evolves between the young sculptor and the beautiful second wife of the *zamindar*, as if to juxtapose as well as accentuate the uncouth lovemaking that takes place between her and her husband.

To conclude, we can say that perhaps Rituparno is hopeful that with time his film will attain the same status as did Aparna Sen's *Paroma*, made way back in 1985 wherein the protagonist, a 40-year-old homemaker falls in love with a man almost half her age. The film caused a lot of hullabaloo among middle-class Bengali cinegoers then, but is now applauded by feminists and ordinary viewers alike as a landmark film depicting the emergence of the 'new woman.'

References

Antarmahal (*Views of the Inner Chamber*). Dir. Rituparno Ghosh. Perf. Jackie Shroff, Abhisekh Bachchan, Soha Ali Khan and Rupa Ganguli. AB Corp. and Puja Films. 2005. Film.

Chakravarti, Paromita, and Ganguly Swati, "Postcolonial Negotiations with the Nation: Rituparno Ghosh's *Chokher Bali*". *The Indian ImagiNation: Colonial and Postcolonial Literature and Culture*. Ed. Somdatta Mandal. New Delhi: Creative Books, 2007: 242–259.

Chatterjee, Shoma A. "Tagore on Celluloid: A Fusion of the Modern and the Postmodern". *Tagore and Modernity*. Eds. Krishna Sen and Tapati Gupta. Kolkata: Dasgupta & Co, 2006: 211–225.

Chokher Bali (*Sand in the Eye*) Dir. Rituparno Ghosh. Perf. Aishwarya Rai, Lili Chakraborty, Prosenjit Chatterjee, Raima Sen, Tota Raychaudhuri. Shri Venkatesh Films. 2003. Film.

Kaplan, Ann E. *Looking For the Other: Feminism, Film and the Imperial Gaze*. New York & London: Routledge, 1997.

Mandal, Somdatta. "Rituparno Ghosh: The 'Woman's' Director of Bengali Cinema." *Films and Feminism*. Eds. Jasbir Jain and Sudha Rai. Jaipur and New Delhi: Rawat Publications, 2002: 17–38.

Mulvey, Laura. "Visual Pleasure and Narrative Cinema." *Screen* 16(3): 6–27. Reprinted in *Visual and Other Pleasures*. London: Macmillan, 1994.

"Q & A Interview with Rituparno Ghosh." April 15, 2005. <*www.asiasource.org/news/special_reports/ghosh.cfm*>

9.
Women's Issues in Telugu Films: Limits of Social Reform

C. VIJAYASREE

Telugu Film industry, the second largest of its kind in India, celebrated its platinum jubilee recently. Conservative estimates indicate that the industry produces around 150 films a year. The corpus of Telugu films is therefore so large that it is hazardous to offer any generalizations about its trends and themes. The one aspect I wish to examine here is the forging of issues related to women in films, and the patterns that appear in the presentation/representation of these issues. I will quickly track here the trajectory of woman-centric films in Telugu and examine the ideological underpinnings of these film texts. This will enable us to determine the discursive shifts in the genre and note if these have made a qualitative difference to the perception and handling of women's issues. To plot this, I shall point to the dominant trends in each decade. Let me add that the analysis is by no means exhaustive; it only focuses on certain nodal issues at different points of time, in the evolution of women's film as a sub-genre in Telugu cinema.

Telugu cinema has always been sensitive to the problems of women and given considerable space to women's issues. It is significant to note that the 30s witnessed the making of some reformist movies such as *Mala Pilla* (The Harijan Girl, 1938) and *Malli Pelli* (Remarriage,1939). Issues such as dowry, child marriage and widow marriage engaged the attention of the film makers through the 50s. The woman, in her familial role as the upholder of tradition, appears insistently in these movies. Titles such as *Devata* (Deity), *Patni* (Wife), *Charanadasi* (Devout Servant), *Kannatalli* (Mother), *Ardhangi* (The Better Half) reveal an underlying pattern – the representation of woman in her roles as mother, wife and daughter was linked to the dominant socio-political discourse of the time. The motive of the early films was to create a national identity. The family acted as a microcosm of the whole system. In the familial sphere, the representation of women in roles defined by their relation to male figures consolidated religious, social and political values.

By the 60s women came to be recognized as playing key roles as audience and consumers of films. Understanding and appealing to a female audience became an important factor for the success or failure of a film. The melodrama genre was designed to appeal to a specifically female audience, with its emotional and sentimental content in the depiction of femininity. Women's issues became subjects of films, not so much for the intrinsic social urgency they demanded, but to attract female audience through sob-stories. Narratives of suffering have always remained popular in the genre of women's films – advertised as *Mahila Chitralu*. A woman's suffering, her sacrifices and the eventual triumph of the divinity in her, constitute the central thematic strand in these movies. These films insistently deify women and re-inscribe the conventional expectations, urging women to conform to them. In these depictions, where patriarchal values are upheld, often mythical characters such as Sita and Savitri are used as role models.

It was in the 60s that professional women made their appearance on the Telugu screen—*Velugu Needalu* (Savithri as doctor) *Manchi Manasulu* (Savithri as lawyer) and *Chaduvukunna Ammayilu* (Educated Girls). Women's education being the key issue, these films play their role in promoting this ideal. But like the nationalist discourse on female education, these films too ensure that the purpose of female education is only to make a woman a better helpmeet for a man. The point I wish to make is that these films keeps to the contours of the dominant discourses of the time even when appear to contest them.

In the 70s, issues such as the travails of a working woman (*Antuleni Katha*, 1976, *Illanta Sandadi*, 1978), suffering of a woman in marriage (*Idi Katha Kadu*, *47 Rojulu*) were popular. Some agency is allowed to women here but it is the suffering of a woman that actually gets highlighted and therefore these films make an addition to the stereotypical sob-stories about women rather than serve as stories about self-reliant women. One of the most successful women's film of the decade is *Manushulu Marali*, which won actress Sarada the 'Urvasi' award. This film typifies the sub-genre of 'Motherhood' films which glorify the role of a self-sacrificing mother often projected as the microcosmic symbol of Mother India. Once again, suffering is portrayed as a value in itself, and a woman's identity is linked to her capacity for suffering—the suffering woman is held up as a model of womanhood, idealized, honoured and venerated.

It was in the 80s that films dealing with women's issues, forging strong women characters and shaping new identities for women were made. Let me begin with two examples here, directed by two innovative, experimental and progressive directors – K.Viswanath and Bapu. In choosing these examples my attempt is not to disparage these early attempts to bring the issue of a loveless marriage and the ways to deal with it under scrutiny. I wish to refer here to an important sub-genre of women's films – 'Films about marriage'. These films do not end with a marriage, after which the couple supposedly lives happily ever after, but begins with one and depicts issues of marital disharmony. The two films I am referring to are *Saptapadi* (1980) and *Radha Kalyanam* (1981). The story line in both these films follows a similar trajectory – a girl forced into a loveless marriage against her choice. In both the cases, the husband gets to know of her earlier affair. In *Saptapadi*, the husband and father-in-law – the latter, a traditional Brahmin Vedic scholar represented as the ideal patriarch, return the girl with ritualistic formalities to her lover—a harijan. In this film, the director, K. Viswanath, has obviously broken all norms of caste, religion and tradition. In *Radha Kalyanam* too the generous husband prepares the ground for a similar grand return. In the climactic scene, however, the lover who obviously believes more in the sanctity of marriage than in the power of love insists that the husband remove the mangalsutra before handing over the girl. Mangalsutra becomes the crux of the issue, and in a scene charged with emotion and sentiment, the husband approaches the girl and tries to snatch the mangalsutra; the girl falls at the feet of her husband, screaming and yelling hysterically. The two films have a dialogic relationship. But what is important is the fact that regardless of the ending chosen in each case, both the films keep the power structures of patriarchy intact. In both cases the woman has no agency. She is the silent object ; the men speak for her. She has neither the agency nor the power to make decisions. Thus in the so-called woman-centric texts too, the deep structures of patriarchy remain unquestioned; and sometimes even get re-forged. To the same genre belongs another big hit by Balachandar – *Mauna Ragam* (1986). In this film, a newly-wed couple file for divorce and the court ordains them to live together for a year before granting it to them. But in this one year the wife is so overwhelmed by the chivalry of her husband that she finds herself completely in love with him and the story ends with a happy union. In all this, the perfectly chivalrous hero gets the lion's share in representation and the woman's suffering in a loveless marriage gets somewhat blurred. In fact, the audience often feels sympathetic towards the hero. All these films display a disconcertingly conservative strain, re-inscribing patriarchy even while trying to contest it.

In the same decade, we have a significant number of films which accords the woman agency for action and sees her spearheading movements for change. This is also the decade of the angry young woman in Telugu cinema. One of the major issues forged in these films is rape and victimization of woman. Physical assault on women has been treated with earnestness in Telugu films. Solutions to this are however stereotypical: the victim either dies, kills the rapist and kills herself or effects a change of heart in the man that assaults her and eventually marries him; in more recent versions a helpful male companion gives her courage and rehabilitates her. In movie after movie, the stigma attached to such an incident is replayed and rehearsed. In case of domestic violence, it is only a sadist that is considered deserving of punishment.

Rape as an issue in cinema dates back to the films of the 60s and 70s. These early representations of rape in films such as *Maro Charitra* (Another History), *Kannevayasu* (The Virgin), *Padaharella Vayasu* (Sweet Sixteen) present women as victims of assault and highlight the suffering which often ends in the death of the heroine. In fact, this theme of a woman as a victim never becomes outdated. It keeps returning with fresh vigour every now and then. In most of these cases, representation of rape leads to an eroticization of rape and the popular attention is therefore diverted not so much towards rape as a crime against women but towards erotic implications of the representation of rape on the screen. As Lynn Higgins and Brenda Silver note – representations of rape in myths and literary texts are at once a structuring device and a gaping elision: "an obsessive inscription — and an obsessive erasure — of sexual violence against women (and by those placed by society in the position of 'woman') ... Over and over ... rape exists as an absence or gap that is both a product and a source of textual anxiety, contradiction, or censorship."(Higgins and Silver: 2–3). The silence, elision and the gap to which Higgins and Silver allude, was a mark of popular Telugu cinema's tradition, notwithstanding its 'obsessive inscription' of rape.

As Jyotika Verdi rightly sums up "As feminists we are caught between a rock and a hard place: the erasure of rape from the narrative bears the mark of a patriarchal discourse on honour and chastity; yet showing rape, some argue, eroticizes it for the male gaze and purveys the victim myth. How do we refuse to erase the palpability of rape and negotiate the splintering of the private/public trauma associated with it?" (Virdi: 30–31).

The eighties' treatment of the subject of rape and exploitation show a different pattern. Retaliating rape victims, who bring the rapist to book, dominate the scene at this time. In other words the avenging woman arrived on the Telugu scene. *Nyayam Kavali* (Justice Wanted, 1981) is a significant moment in the rape-revenge-punishment pattern of response. It is indeed useful to recall that this film was made in the wake of some gory incidents of rape reported around that time. In 1979, the Supreme Court overturned a High Court ruling and freed two police constables accused of raping Mathura, a minor, in police custody. In 1978, a Muslim woman, Rameeza Bee was raped in police custody in Hyderabad and her husband, a rickshaw puller, was murdered for protesting against it. In 1980, Maya Tyagi was raped in Baghpat, Haryana, then stripped naked and made to walk through the streets by the police. The 'rape bill' — the upshot of public shock and women's rage — became the Anti-Rape Act in 1986 (Kumar, 1994). *Nyayam Kavali* examines the ramifications of rape—the fact that rape is nothing but an assertion of male aggression and shows two women, both victims of such aggression, bringing the culprit to court. It demonstrates how harrowing it is for a woman to talk about this debilitating experience. The film truly centers on a woman's narrative. Here Sarada plays the role of a female lawyer who is herself a rape victim and explains to her client how difficult it is to prove guilt in a rape case; for a woman, a court case involving rape is as terrible as the experience of rape itself. Here, it is the women who fight against the injustice – not a boy friend, or some generous police officer. The shift of agency to the woman is significant.

Following this, the 80s saw several avenging heroines. In *Pratighatana* (The Revolt, 1986), the heroine is disrobed in public for having testified against a political leader. The family does not accept her and hence she moves out to live on her own. She then carefully designs and executes a plan through which towards the end of the film, in a violent act of revolt, she publicly hacks to death, her tormenter who is also a menace to society. Another film, *Kartavyam* (Duty), followed the story of a conscientious woman police officer, inspired by the success story of Kiran Bedi. In another powerful woman-centric film of the early 90s,

Ankuram (Seedling), the newly-wed heroine on her way to her husband's home meets with a strange situation. A man being chased by the police leaves his child in her custody and disappears. She reaches her husband's home with a baby in arms and obviously, she is not welcome. The heroic fight put up by the young girl for the principles she believes in constitutes the central thread of the story. There are indeed several stories like this. The point to be noted is that when women fight for a public issue or stage their fight in the public space, they are easily allowed their agency, their heroism and their resistance. The images of women etched out in such situations are clearly marked by autonomy, courage and self-assertion. But the problem arises when the fight is staged in the familial arena. No decisive battles are won here; fundamentals of patriarchy remain untouched. Women here can only take as much democratic space as patriarchy allows.

Issues such as rape and domestic violence, autonomy of women, equality of men and women, creation of a democratic space in the family have engaged the attention of film makers and appealed to the film audience. However, in all these formulations of reform, the discourse rarely challenges the basic structures of patriarchy. Reform often sets its own limits and refuses to disturb the deep structures of the patriarchal culture. We could now look at a successful film of the nineties, *Mr Pellam* (1993), directed by Bapu. The film deals with the reversal of roles in a middle class family, that is for a while, the woman becomes the breadwinner and the man the homemaker under some strange circumstances. This reversal, however, does not change the place or the value, accorded to man and woman on the basis of hierarchy of genders in patriarchy. The man is still the boss. The director uses irony to point out the shallowness of the myth of male superiority. The outer frame comes from the myth: Lakshmi at the feet of Narayana who is reclining on his serpent bed. In the first half, the heroine, significantly named Jhansi, is shown doing the household chores, in a home where the man reigns supreme. Later when the man is suspended from his job owing to being implicated in a case of misappropriation of bank money, she finds a good job where her common sense as a homemaker stands her in good stead and she soon climbs to a managerial position. This does not alter her position at home very much. She takes every care not to ruffle her husband's male ego. Once again there is a brief snap from Lakshmi-Narayana where Lakshmi suggests to her husband a change of place. Narayana granting that, makes sure that Lakshmi is still at his feet. No revolutionary changes occur except that the husband by the end of the story is able to acknowledge his wife's capabilities. However, the domestic status quo does not change. The film takes a dig at the meaningless male ego many men cherish with care, but eventually sees no hope for any change in the domestic space.

Let us now address the question of female identity in these films. A woman can forge an identity of her own when she excels in some field or the other. It could be a cop as in the case of *Vyjayanti IPS* or a successful dancer as in the case of *Mayuri*, the story of Sudha Chandran, or a great singer as in the case of *Sindhu Bhairavi*. While the achievements of women are highlighted here, such exceptions will never make a rule. Autonomy or emancipation of an average woman seems to be still ignored in cinema.

When we turn to the last decade of the twentieth century, there is by and large, a silence about women's issues. One wonders if all battles for women have been won for all time. There is a visible dip in the woman-centric films since the 90s. The new market economy, creation of larger-than-life mega heroes, and perhaps a certain degree of backlash against feminism could have been responsible for this. Even a casual look at the titles of some of the successful movies of the last decade points to the ascendance of all-powerful heroes—*Shankar Dada, Pokiri, Jagapathi, Hitler, Stalin, Jai Chiranjeeva, Bunny, Chatrapathi, Athadu, Anji, Badri, Murari, Daddy, Narasimha, Rakhi, Lakshmi, Gouri* and so on. Big heroes spare no space to strong women; they need typical damsels in distress to enable them to realize their heroism. In terms of representation of women, Telugu films of the last decade have in fact been retrogressive. Films representing politics of transformation in matters of gender and forging feminist agency are yet to make their appearance in Telugu cinema despite the fact that Telugu cinema has always shown an abiding interest and serious preoccupation with women's issues. The emergence of the feminist film in Telugu appears to have suffered a set back in the 21st century and women's issues no longer seem to matter much in a world dominated by 'He-men'. As films became glossier and more hi-tech, the heroes took centre stage and the heroines became mere appendages – they mainly provided glamour. It is imperative to stall this trend before one can hope to see anything like genuine articulation of female consciousness on the Telugu silver screen. Writing in *G*, an Indian film magazine, Monica Motwani states, "The heroine may have metamorphised (sic) over the years, but she still cannot break away from the shackles of certain norms set by Hindi cinema years ago." This is amply true of women in Telugu cinema as well.

References

Higgins, Lynn and Silver, Brenda. Introduction. *Rape and Representation*. Ed. in Lynn Higgins and Brenda Silver. New York: Columbia University Press, 1991: 2–3.

Kumar, Radha. *The History of Doing: An Illustrated Account of Movements for Women's Rights and Feminism in India, 1800–1900*. New Delhi: Kali for Women, 1993.

Motwani, Monica. "The Changing face of the Hindi Film heroine". *G Magazine Online*. 1996.

Virdi, Jyotika. "Reverence, Rape — and then Revenge: Popular Hindi Cinema's Woman's Film". *Screen* Vol. 40. 1999.

10.
A Case Study of the Reel life 'Wimin' in *Fire* and *Girlfriend*: Fruition to Miso phallicism from mere Feminism

SHREE DEEPA

"The cinema is not an art which films life: the cinema is something between art and life. Unlike painting and literature, the cinema both gives to life and takes from it..."

Jean-Luc Godard

The words wo**man** and wo**men** have intrinsically interwoven masculinity in them and scream out that a lady is incomplete without the other gender **'in'** her, and if she ever dared to reject, she is left with nothing but **wo**es. The terms are to be recognized and accepted as derivatives of a 'phallogocentric' society.

A new vocabulary that has arisen from many feminist movements will help us in redefining the role of modern human beings in a liberated society. 'Wimin' 'womin,' 'womyn' are terms produced by many parts of lesbian feminist movements to distinguish it from men and masculine (or 'phallogocentric') language. I choose to derive from this vocabulary in this paper. 'Wimin' are people who consciously reject men from their lives and choose to live their own lives free from the binding shackles of the dominant **man (men) made** society and cultures. They feel, find, and enjoy completeness bereft of the other gender.

Feminism as a philosophy is a shift of focus to women from men, to prove that women matter too. Gynocentrism is a focus on women as a clan and their views and experiences, needs, desires, likes, dislikes, usually without consideration of the other gender's views. Ultra-feminism (caused by both internal and external factors) can give birth to misogamy. It can at times grow into miso-phallicism and become synonymous. Contrary to the male views, miso-phallicism is a result of a woman's life experiences and is not usually congenital.

Mass media, particularly, popular cinema plays a very important role in establishing a didactic purpose or creating a catharsis for the oft-oppressed, ignored, abused gender; the woman becomes *vis a vis* a female or *vice versa*. Two bold films made in India that explores these facets of the Indian woman against the global and the humane backdrop, are considered for discussion in this paper.

The first film *Fire* (1996) by Deepa Mehta and the second *Girl Friend* (2004) by Karan Razdan unflinchingly portray the externally and, internally infused confusion, and the inner strength and conviction, of the 'wimin' in two different lights. The differences (and similarities) are striking and hard to ignore, probably, because of the difference in the gender of the two directors who made the two films. The protagonist characters in both the films, initially show shades of feminism and progress to being gynocentric, then mature to misogyny and eventually end up as miso phallicists with just one exception, Sapna (Amrita Arora) in *Girl Friend*. My attempt in this article is to track this thread of progress in the Indian reel 'womyn' contemporary or otherwise; emancipated or bound; in these two bold movies that have been laudably made in India. Neither moral angle, nor religion, nor conventional philosophies can help us here, but a humane approach alone needs to be adapted in an effort to criticise objectively.

The story of the first film *Fire* centres around a newly-wed couple (Javed Jaffery and Nandita Das) and an older couple (Shabana Azmi and Kulbhushan Kharbanda). Both the husbands neglect their duty towards their wives for various reasons. The two women (read female door-mats) become feminists. They start finding emotional comfort in each other and in serving their mother-in-law, Biji. They progress into being gynocentric, where they realize that their opinions must matter. The deftly written dialogues stir and tug at the heart strings of every Indian woman.

> Sita: Isn't it amazing? We're so bound by customs and rituals. Somebody just has to press my button, this button marked Tradition, and I start responding like a trained monkey. Do I shock you?

Radha: Yes.

Sita: You're lovely.

The inner quest for freedom from forced submission to the unloving men slowly ticks like a time bomb and the women become more gynocentric with each frame. This is when they have their first unplanned emotionally driven sexual encounter with each other. It is adeptly handled by the director, a woman, and all obscenity is carefully avoided or masked. It is in no sense pornographic.

Newly wed Sita (Nandita Das) has her modest dreams just like any Indian girl. Trapped in a loveless, arranged marriage in which her husband keeps only his mistress's picture in his wallet, she sees little hope for happiness. She comes across as a gynocentric person at this juncture. Her rebellious dialogues authenticate this claim. This is where their feminism matures into gynocentrism. Sita's gynocentric behaviour rubs off on Radha as well who is used to being a lesser creature than a mere female, because her husband uses her as an object to prove his celibate self control.

Radha's reverberating words 'no eggs' to signify her barrenness clearly demonstrate that women in this family are baby-making machines. From being less than a female, she learns quickly from the very intelligent Sita and metamorphoses into a feminist and later a misogamist. When these women become 'wimin', misogamy sets in very slowly but surely. They stop caring about their husbands and stop putting the husbands' needs before theirs. The reason for such a change is not the 'wimin' themselves but the uncaring, emotionless, ever-demanding men in the movie. This is a lesson for all men who choose to ignore their wives for whatever reasons. The dialogues between Jatin and Sita support this claim.

Sita: Are you coming home tonight?

Jatin: Maybe.

Radha: Where's Jatin?

Sita: Meeting his girlfriend.

Misogamy is at its peak when both the wives refuse to satiate their husbands who feel that they must be satisfied as it is their right as husbands and not because they love their respective wives. Sita's role during consummation, as a wife is animalistic; she is emotionless and romanceless as she treats it as a chore. It happens because Sita must have a baby. The ever-evading baby is a powerful symbol at two levels in this film. First, its absence in the egg form in Radha's body robs her of her sexual pleasures. Radha is infertile. This drives her husband to follow a guru who advocates resisting temptation. He does resist and the marriage has been celibate for thirteen years. With their husbands' attentions elsewhere, the sisters-in-law must become misogamists, being locked in unrewarding marriages. Radha even begins to assert herself with her husband. Clearly, the domestic set-up grows unendurable by the minute. The sisters-in-law turn to each other for emotional support. Their realization that the Indian language lacks a word for their relationship, literally sets the ball rolling for the Indian audience. The truth is that there is no word for lesbianism in any of the Indian languages. This is when a philosophical dimension for sexual orientation is opened.

> Sita: There is no word in our language that can describe us and how we feel for each other.

It is of course the Indian context that gives this naïve story its resonance. The men are more confused and shocked than threatened. Sita and Radha start more clearly. Since their lives have been made empty, pointless and frustrating by their husbands who see them as breeding stock or as unpaid employees. Seeing things, they must break free and 'live' a life of fulfilment; a life that is their own. The two women are very beautiful and the movie is all about their journey from being female to misogamists and finally to miso phallicists. The film has a seductive reverberation. It gently highlights that women are from Venus and men are from Mars.

Deepa Mehta's *Fire* is a plea for women's self-determination. But the reasons for such a deliberate journey are clearly portrayed by Mehta because, initially these women are introduced as 'normal straight' women, but are forced to turn into 'wimin' by men. The message is clear, if the men want to be a part of the women's lives, they must contribute productively to the marriage, if they fail their wives become 'wimin'. Biji (Kushal Rekhi), who after a major stroke does 'no talking but much listening' is one of the central characters. In the most shocking scene in the film, their servant Mundu (Ranjit Chowdhary) masturbates within a few yards of Biji, treating her like a piece of furniture. But the family matriarch Biji, rendered silent by a stroke, is the embodiment of the old order weakened but still very much present. She is not a part of the modern 'wimin' but clearly a female who wants no part in the 'wiminhood'. She spits on the face of Radha when she comes to know of the audacity and the lesbian 'fling', but surprisingly, she does not do similar with contempt to her servant Mundu.

The title of the movie comes from the Indian legend where Lord Rama tests the purity of his wife through a fire test. This bit of mythology is a major element in the film's conclusion. We are also treated to repeated lyrical and colourful flashbacks of a childhood family outing. The film's argument, that life without passion is pointless, is summed up in a speech that Radha delivers to her husband near the conclusion. Mercifully, the two lovers are united by the woman director and script writer in the end when the credits roll, where Radha survives the 'Fire' test of purity and is a complete miso phallicist. We do hope the two wimin live happily ever after.

In the film *Girlfriend* we have two women characters, who are introduced as 'wimin' and their hatred for man as a gender is very clear from the very outset, unlike in the movie *Fire*. Tanya (Isha Koppikar) is a clear miso phallicist and an obvious Butch, while Sapna (Amrita Arora) a Femme is more 'phallic-phobic'. These are not 'normal straight' women in the introduction and many dialogues and incidences in the film prove this point. However, the director might have had a problem internalising the concept of lesbianism and this might have induced him to introduce a so-called saviour in the form of a man, Rahul (Aashish Chowdhary). Rahul, the redeemer ironically introduces himself as a gay and dupes Sapna into believing that she is safe with him, in the absence of the ever protective and loving Tanya. Strangely, Sapna falls in love with him. Rahul becomes the self proclaimed liberator of Sapna and he feels it is his mission to save her from 'Tanya's Jungle' (read lesbianism) and their 'strange friendship'.

Incidentally, Sapna is an orphan and all her needs – food, shelter and clothing are taken care of by Tanya, who also physically wrestles with men in the ring at nights to make some extra money. Tanya calls her girl 'baccha,' 'baabu,' 'baby,' and 'janam' with a lot of love. She is deeply in love with Sapna. They have just one physical encounter with each other when drunk, after which Sapna requests Tanya not to let the episode repeat itself and prefers not to remember the incident. Tanya keeps this promise. Sapna too seems to be in love with Tanya although she does not dare to acknowledge it in the movie. However, she remarks to Rahul "I never liked boys till I met you" and "Why do all good looking men have to be gay?"

The twist in the tale happens when the two girls and the guy form a unique love triangle. The male director has a message for the audience, lesbian or otherwise. The miso phallicist Tanya, who maintains her stance (dictated by her childhood abuse and molestation), in spite of the societal dictates or Rahul's advice that she must "get a life partner" (read get married to a guy) grows mad and becomes a lunatic. The message is, if you are a lesbian and hate men, you will become mad, and your girl will marry a man given half a chance. In one of the scenes Rahul remarks "men fall in love with women, not men." The concept of lesbianism is thoroughly rejected by the director and script writer.

The director cruelly snatches Sapna away from Tanya and hands her over to Rahul, thus achieving the phallic purpose that women are made for men to enjoy. He also makes Sapna mouth many acidic abuses, such as "You are a bloody Les....." and "You are a witch", when she comes to know that it was Tanya who tried to distance her from Rahul. Sapna refuses to even say the word "Lesbian" completely and stops half way. Perhaps, these are not Sapna's words but the male director's words. To him a lesbian is not supposed to be happy. The lesbian character in *Girlfriend* becomes increasingly possessive about her partner and becomes psychopathic as the film reaches its conclusion.

The film's director, Karan Razdan, said the movie was about a woman who becomes a lesbian due to her circumstances rather than her sexual orientation at birth. ''I have not made a pro-lesbian film but my film has started a debate about the subject," he said. "Whether my film generates good or bad publicity, my intention is to start a discussion about this subject, and create awareness in society", he adds. This awareness is phallic in its portrayal because after a prolonged fight between Rahul and Tanya for Sapna, Tanya is made to jump off the window and fall to her death. Since the director is a man, her death is imminent for uttering words like "Men make you cry," "All guys are unfaithful," "You do not know about these men," "I hate these men, stay away from them," "The result of falling in love with a boy — tension, problems, not worth it!" and finally "We don't need men!"

Sapna, unable to heave her heart into her mouth, just utters Tanya's name as Tanya falls to her death. The dead body is grotesque but, not a true, loving tear flows nor is a word of mourning uttered. Her death is the death of a lesbian no doubt, but seems more a punishment for being a miso phallicist. Sapna is saved, for she is normal and takes to the arms of a man and mends her ways to become straight.

The concept of lesbianism is treated differently in both the movies and the 'wimin' are different too. In the first movie *Fire* the two protagonists, initially straight women are voluntarily 'converted lesbians'. The reason for this conversion is elaborately portrayed and described step by step. The entire show is full of femininity, and lesbianism crafts itself as a solution to their problems. The society in *Fire* scorns this unlabelled relationship, but the 'wimin' are complete. This story has a happy ending and promises a great future for these 'wimin'. But in the second movie *Girlfriend* both the 'wimin' are miso phallicists. Tanya is killed for refusing to revamp and mend her ways. Sapna is allowed to live as she learns the lessons taught by the male director and turns straight. Strangely, the society in this film has not much to do with the didactic purpose, because many incidents are pictured around gays, lesbians and their bars and parties, with an exception of Rahul, whose sole purpose in the film is to change the orientation of Sapna.

Both the movies evoked much public scorn. The Indian audience failed to acknowledge and respect the human rights of lesbians. It is interesting to note that these relationships were till very recently against the law in India. Article 377 of the Indian Penal Code confirms this point.

It is also interesting to note that the Indian languages lack the word lesbian and the English language lacks the words miso phallicist, miso phallicism or miso phallic, whereas misogyny is an oft-used word. Though we have misandry as an alternate word, it is insufficient to completely describe the contempt that the miso phallicists have. In other words the language favours men and give men the permission to hate women, but, 'wimin' do not have such a privilege even at a word level, let alone in practical life. The limit for the 'wimin' is just misogamy (usually used by gays and occasionally used by women). Society needs to wake up to this reality and start respecting women for what they are and allow them to be what they want to be. Whether Feminism or Gynocentricism or Misogamy or Miso phallicism—women must assert their rights and progress in spite of the phallic hurdles.

References

Butler, Judith. "Imitation and Gender Insubordination." *Inside/Out: Lesbian Theories, Gay Theories*. ed. Diana Fuss. New York: Routledge, 1991. (reprinted in *The Lesbian and Gay Studies Reader*. eds. Abelove et al. New York: Routledge, 1993: 307–320).

Case, Sue-Ellen. "Towards a Butch-Femme Aesthetic." Discourse 11 (Winter 1988–1989). (reprinted in *The Lesbian and Gay Studies Reader*. eds. Abelove et al. New York: Routledge, 1993: 294–306).

Davis, Madeline, and E. L. Kennedy. "'They was no one to mess with': The Construction of the Butch Role in the Lesbian Community of the 1940's and 1950's." *The Persistent Desire: A Femme-Butch Reader*. ed. Joan Nestle. Boston: Alyson, 1992: 62–79.

de Lauretis, Teresa. "Sexual Indifference and Lesbian Representation." Theatre Journal 40 (1988). (reprinted in *The Lesbian and Gay Studies Reader*. eds. Abelove et al. New York: Routledge, 1993: 141–158).

Fire. Dir. Deepa Mehta. Perf. Shabana Azmi, Kulbhushan Kharbanda, Nandita Das, Javeed Jaffery. Kaleidoscope Entertainment Pvt. Ltd. 1996. Film.

Girlfriend. Dir. Karan Razdan. Perf. Aashish Chaudhary, Amrita Arora and Ishaa Koppikar. Pammi Baweja. 2004. Film.

Jeffreys, Sheila. *The Spinster and Her Enemies: Feminism and Sexuality*, 1880-1930; Spinifex, Reprint 1987.

Nestle, Joan. "Butch-Femme Relationships: Sexual Courage in the 1950's." Heresies 12 (1981). (reprinted in Joan Nestle, A Restricted Country. Ithaca, NY: Firebrand, 1987: 100–109).

Newton, Esther. "The Mythic Mannish Lesbian: Radclyffe Hall and the New Woman." Signs 9.4 (Summer 1984). (reprinted in Hidden from History: Reclaiming the Gay and Lesbian Past. eds. Martin Duberman et al. New York: NAL Books, 1989: 281–293).

Rich, Adrienne. "Compulsory Heterosexuality and Lesbian Existence." Signs 5 (1980). (reprinted in *The Lesbian and Gay Studies Reader*. eds. Abelove et al. New York: Routledge, 1993: 227–254).

Smith-Rosenberg, Carroll. "Discourses of Sexuality and Subjectivity: The New Woman, 1870-1936." *Disorderly Conduct: Visions of Gender in Victorian America*. New York: Alfred A. Knopf, 1985. New York: Penguin, 1989: 264–280.

Websites Visited

http://en.wikipedia.org/wiki/Lesbian_feminism

http://www.imdb.com/Reviews/100/10092

http://www.imdb.com/title/tt0116308/externalreviews

http://www.imdb.com/title/tt0116308/quotes

http://news.bbc.co.uk/go/pr/fr/-/2/hi/entertainment/3805905.stm.

http://rogerebert.suntimes.com/apps/pbcs.dll/article?AID=/19970919/REVIEWS/709190302/1023

http://www.sfgate.com/cgi-bin/article.cgi?f=/c/a/1997/09/26/DD60969.DTL

http://www.shoestring.org/mmi_revs/fire96.html

http://home.snafu.de/fablab/queerview/500er/513fire/english513.htm

http://www.sodomylaws.org/world/india/innews049.htm

http://www.imdb.com/Reviews/91/9193

http://en.wikipedia.org/wiki/Gynocentrism

http://en.wikipedia.org/wiki/Lesbian_feminism#Womyn.27s_culture

11.
Gender @ Cyberspace: Who's Online?

LAVANYA KOLLURI

What is perhaps central to the debate on women in media is the question of how completely a woman is identified with her body and how limited she is to her gender. When we talk about women, the subtext is usually the body. Critical discourse on the representation of women in media invariably focuses on how her body is represented. And when we say the media is sexist or insensitive, it is the treatment of women's bodies that we are troubled by. Therefore, the site on which my paper is built is primarily the body. However, in a polemical sleight of hand, I intend to make the body disappear and explore how gender is construed.

Discourses surrounding the body often hinge on the classic binary of sex: male and female. But how real is this binary? Tracing its origins, Thomas Laqueur, in his extensively researched book, *Making Sex: Body and Gender from the Greeks to Freud*, shows how our concept of the body has evolved from the one-sex to the two-sex model. Examining medical and philosophical literature, and accounts from reproductive anatomy and physiology from the second century A.D. down to the twentieth century, he shows how descriptions of the body were used by scientists, political activists, literary figures and theorists to explain gender. In the one-sex model, prevalent from antiquity to the early seventeenth century, man was the only sex and woman was merely an inversion of this basic form. Her bodily differences served the specific purposes culture ordained for her. From the eighteenth century onwards, the two-sex model was in vogue; reproductive organs became the "foundation of incommensurable differences" and sex became the "primary foundational category differentiating men and women" (Laqueur: 69).

In the light of this pivotal position of the body in understanding gender today, this paper examines whether the absence of the body, as a defining element of gender, would change the hue of the discourse. I propose to explore a specific media space that supposedly does away with the body — cyberspace — and to engage, dialectically, with the possibility that the absence of the body may allow for radically different representations of gender.

I begin with an article titled "The Strange Case of the Electronic Lover" that appeared in *Ms. Magazine* in 1991. It recounts the story of Joan Green, a young woman who due to an accident has paralysis, disfigurement and speech disability. She entered an all-woman chat programme seeking companionship. Over a period of three years she underwent a gradual transformation – from a suicidal recluse, she became a socially confident woman, setting up a women's discussion group and inspiring other women in the chat room to deal with a range of psychological problems. However, she suddenly developed a life-threatening disease and it appeared that she was going to die. After a huge outpouring of grief from the women in the chat programme, she miraculously recovered and then revealed the truth about herself: Joan was actually Alex, an American psychiatrist in his fifties. He had once entered the chat room using the name (called 'handle' in chat programmes) Shrink Inc., curious to see how women interacted online. He was mistaken for a woman and soon found that other women began confiding in him. So he created this persona called Joan.

Interestingly, most of the women in the chat programme felt betrayed by the disclosure of the truth. For them, Joan was a very real person, their best friend, and most of them felt that Alex should not have told the truth! This is one of the most publicized examples of gender-swapping on the Internet. The question it raises is pertinent to the thrust of this paper. Since the body and its physical attributes were not the basis on which the women assumed Joan was female, is gender constructed by other means in online interactions?

Online communication is marked by the absence of the usual verbal, visual and aural cues for understanding and responding to others in interaction. Online interactions are obviously not as information-rich as face-to-face interactions. Does online communication then, rely on other channels, thereby opening up new possibilities for self-expression? Cyberspace is often celebrated as an emancipatory space by cyberfeminists (Turkle, Haraway, Plant, and Braidotti) because physical markers such as sex, race, body type and size are not obviously discernible in this space and therefore not relevant for categorizations of self/other. The prediction is that, free of corporeal experience, the mind in cyberspace will generate new forms for rendering the self and the other, and for organizing interpersonal communication. Cyberspace offers, as Allucquere Roseanne Stone puts it:

> ... potential for emergent behavior, for new social forms that arise in circumstances in which 'body', 'meeting', 'place', and even 'space' mean things quite different from our accustomed understanding ... How do groups of friends evolve when their meeting room exists in purely symbolic space? How does narrowing the bandwidth — that is, doing without the customary modes of symbolic exchange such as gesture and tone of voice — affect sharing and trust? How do inhabitants of virtual systems construct and maintain categories such as gender and race? (Stone: 610)

Cyberspace – the new frontier for interaction and expression — heralds the crossing and erasure of boundaries imposed by physicality. Categories of difference that 'constrain' everyday, face-to-face interaction will not matter in cyberspace, proclaim its enthusiasts, because they will not be apparent online. Identity will no longer be construed through sex, age and physical appearance. Instead, we can choose the identity we wish to project, whether through email, chat programmes, instant messengers, or virtual communities. Computer-mediated communication facilitates not just instantaneous interaction with geographically distant people, but also the possibilities of travelling through electronic space, as someone other than the person manifest through our bodies.

A person's online characterizations may not even 'match' his/her physical attributes. Where then, do we locate identity? While the creation of multiple selves is not something new, or exclusive to cyberspace, the notion of multiple selves that have no awareness of one another is certainly a radical way of thinking about social interaction. Stone calls this the 'metaphysics of presence' — an overarching consciousness that sorts and organizes our experiences despite the multiple selves of online personae.

Now, if cyberspace is the nebulous, gender-free medium that it is made out to be, do the texts created on it reflect this? In the first place, communication and identity formation in cyberspace rely heavily on text. Because physical cues are not available, online conversants must communicate everything that they want others to know about them through text. Transcribing a complex, nuanced range of attributes (physical, social, psychological and gender-related) into text that can be typed out rapidly is a complex achievement (Turkle: 59). And, since not everyone online may be capable of such nuanced and complex representations, what probably happens is that they take recourse to offline stereotypes.

In presenting the self to others in electronic interactions, the easy way out for people not comfortable with the text-intensive nature of computer-mediated communication, would be to rely on stereotypes, especially those that are likely to elicit desirable responses. It is common experience that on chat and instant messenger programmes female-sounding names, especially those of popular models or film stars elicit more responses than male ones.

It is not surprising, therefore, to find that even in this gender-amorphous space, gender identity is very visible. This could be as innocuous as online forms (on websites, online communities, and email) that routinely ask for gender identity. Or as gross as the hyper-gendering one finds on virtual realties (online role-playing games) where Aishwarya or Cindy Crawford are the 'ideal' handles, thus perhaps carrying over stereotypes from the real world. Internet pornography is the most visible site where offline stereotypes about sexuality are carried over online. Further, as Judy Wajcman points, it is men who gender-swap more frequently on cyberspace, which suggests that the ability to switch identities could very easily be another weapon of power that men may have over women.

Statistics of women's presence on the web are also dismal (Bimber). websites by men far outnumber those by women and male users far outnumber female users. The average Internet user is often described as "a white, middle-aged, educated male". On most online discussion groups, women lurk rather than actually post messages. However, the statistics are changing. More and more women are taking to the Net and enabling the development of distinctive, feminine voices in cyberspace.

The early days of the World Wide Web held promise of an online women's publishing revolution, as an alternative to the viciously male-dominated offline publishing industry, with a flurry of websites focussing on the many aspects of women's lives (like www.oxygen.com, www.iVillage.com). Creating a home page – "a real estate metaphor of the self" – to use Turkle's phrase, allowed women to express themselves and reach out to other women. Today, these sites seem to feature mainly beauty, health, homemaking tips, and horoscopes rather than intellectual topics, for which, women seem to visit the same sites as men: Google, Yahoo, etcetera. What then, have these websites for women achieved? The strongest contribution of these sites is not so much their 'intellectual strength' as a creating sense of community (Brown). These online communities have opened up spaces for women to talk to each other and share information, knowledge and experience.

Online journals, e-zines and blogs are other sites in cyberspace where women's voices and views are increasingly being heard, creating a space not easily available in the offline world, because traditional academic writing is governed by the norms of institutional policy and the political practices of universities and academic journals. As Sefcovic and Bifano point out:

> ... the academic tradition in most disciplines evolved in tandem with a masculine style of academic writing that is highly structured, uses linguistic conventions that purport to be objective while establishing hierarchical differences between researcher and human subjects and lay audiences.

Feminist research, on the other hand, often examines how social knowledge is produced, and seeks to challenge dominant discourses. Its primary, though not only, method is qualitative, with data including narratives, stories, objects, or artifacts that are traditionally ignored (Sefcovic and Bifano). Online journals offer opportunities for such research; women are increasingly using this space to articulate their voices in ways that would not perhaps be possible with the masculine bias of academic print journals. One example from an online journal should serve to illustrate this point.

"The Cyborg Mother: A Breached Boundary", an article in the online journal *CTheory.net*, recounts a single mother's experiences of watching her three-and-a-half- month old premature baby in an incubator. It is written partly in the autobiographical mode, with journal-like passages describing her baby in the incubator interspersed with reflections on what it means to be the biological mother of a cyborg. An extract from the text illustrates this:

> March 30, 2003 – Quinn has been fighting with her ventilator. She tries to tug it out of her throat, but it's glued to her skin. To

> stop her from wrestling, the doctor drugged her with sedatives and paralyzed her so she can't move, so the ventilator can fully take over her body. How can such violence give life? So, I read her a story by Dr. Seuss about really small people called Whos... At the sound of my voice, she opened her eyes for a minute. That's not supposed to happen. I was asked to leave. I was disrupting the machine.
>
> Living within a mediated body means that rituals of being are also written by technology. Technology is mimesis, the capability of imitating the human condition with such exactitude that it has become synonymous with the skin, the flesh, the vital organs of human bodies. Artificial life becomes the performance of real life. Distinguishing between skin and machine thus becomes difficult.

What we see here is a woman's personal narrative of motherhood juxtaposed with an analysis of how technology can mediate the symbiotic relation between mother and child. The juxtaposition of the textual styles — journal entries and prosaic analysis — echoes the human-technology interface, the cyborg. But the article is not a dispassionate or rigidly theoretical analysis of cyborg consciousness. Nor does it use the popular cyberpunk motif of the cyborg as seen in films like *The Matrix* and *Bladerunner* or novels like *Neuromancer*, where cyborg women are techno-eroticized bodies serving the love/lust angle of the male protagonists. Instead, personal – autobiographical narrative is wedded to analytical reflection that throws up a more feminine, more personalized description of the cyborg. Texts like these encourage us to think of cyberspace as the threshold of new and important re-locations for cultural practice, highlighting its potential for creative solutions.

In the final analysis, how do we evaluate this exciting, new space — cyberspace? Clearly, many of the old stereotypes from the real world are spilling over into the virtual world. And the gender-gap in terms of access to cyberspace is also very real. As Braidotti points out, it takes more than just technology to really alter patterns of thought and mental habits, and unless we can take up the challenge and invent suitably new forms of expression, this technology might just prove to be useless or worse still, may perpetuate existing gender biases. It remains to be seen how women will take up the challenge.

References

Bimber, Bruce. "Measuring the Gender Gap on the Internet." 24 Aug. 2003. *Social Science Quarterly* 81:3 (2000). 20 Jan. 2007. <http://www.personal.si.umich.edu/~rfrost/courses/SI110/readings/DigiDivide/BimberonDigiDivide.pdf>

Braidotti, Rosa. "Cyberfiminism with a Difference." 3 July, 1996. *Universitat Utrecht*. 20 Jan. 2007 <http://www.let.uu.nl/womens_studies/rosi/cyberfem.htm>

Brown, Jenelle. "What happened to the Women's Web?" *Salon.com*. 25 Aug. 2000. <http://archive.salon.com/tech/feature/2000/08/25/womens_web/print.html>

Gibson, William. *Neuromancer*. New York: Ace, 1984.

Haraway, Donna. *Simians, Cyborgs and Women: The Reinvention of Nature.* Routledge: London and New York, 1991.

Gelder Lindsay van, "The Strange Case of the Electronic Lover". *Ms. Magazine*, October 365 (1985). August 2003. 6 Jan, 2007. <www.sscnet.ucla.edu>

Plant, Sadie. Zeroes and Ones: *Digital Women and the New Technoculture*. New York: Doubleday, 1997.

Sefcovic, Enid M.I. and Bifano, Diane Theresa. "Creating a Rhetorical Home for Feminists in the 'Master's House' of the Academy: Toward a Gendered Taxonomy of Form and Content." *Women and Language*. 27 (2004) Questia – The Online Library of Books and Journals. 20 Jan. 2007. <www.questia.com>

Stone, Allucquere Roseanne. 1992. "Virtual Systems." *Incorporations*. Ed. J. Crary and S. Kwinter. New York: ZONE, 1992.

Turkle, Shelley. *Life on the Screen: Identity in the Age of the Internet*. New York: Simon and Schuster, 1995.

Wajcman, Judy. *Feminism Confronts Technology*. Cambridge, England: Polity. 1991.

Windsor, JaimieSmith. "The Cyborg Mother: A Breached Boundary." 2 April,2004. *CTheory.Net*. 2 Jan. 2007. < http://www.ctheory.net/articles.aspx?id=409>

12.
Women in Media: The Politics of Representation

SAUMYA GARIMA JAIPURIAR

In this article, I will be focusing on the representation of women in crime-stories in mainstream English newspapers and to what extent these are reflective of a deeper social position which itself is constituted of various contradictory attitudes; neo-conservative as well as radical.

The cases of Jessica Lal and Priyadarshini Mattoo have brought to the fore, discussions about the representation of women in media reports. The crimes committed against these women are not just rape and/or murder, but also delayed justice and media reporting. Even at its most sympathetic, the mainstream English print media has been blind and insensitive to certain gender issues. It does not understand for example that bringing crime against women to public notice is as important as the ideological/theoretical underpinning of the exercise. Through my paper I would like to explore this with special reference to the Lal and Mattoo cases. I would also like to look at how continued media focus may inadvertently help in perpetuating a discourse of oppression, by deflecting attention from the real issues to peripheral ones, which in turn may indirectly support a conservative approach to gender matters.

The story of the Jessica Lal case goes as far back as eight years. She was shot dead on April 29, 1999. The media has been congratulated for whipping up public interest in this case and mobilizing popular support to reopen the case. The judicial activism that was seen in this case has also been linked to the efforts of the media. On the surface it is indeed difficult to find fault with the media, for it seemed to portray the case in a sympathetic light. But certain things remain unaccounted for. The choice of the illustration to go with the report is at once noticeable. In around 90% of the reports a photograph of Jessica accompanied the report. The effect of a visual cue is immense in constructing meaning and assigning identities. A picture, as they say, speaks a thousand words. The oft-reprinted photograph of Jessica, in a particularly model-like pose, emphasizes her profession, thereby assigning in an indirect way a cause-effect relationship between her profession and her murder. Though it is tempting to dismiss this line of argument as mere fanciful over-reading, it is nevertheless pertinent to note that such associative reading is an established idea in media and considerable editorial work goes into the use of graphics and photographs. The photograph of Jessica undercut the apparent gender sensitivity of the reports that it accompanied. It perpetuated gender stereotypes and presented a counter point to the woman-as-innocent-victim trope suggested by the reports. What we get then is the depiction of crime as intimately related to the victim's social life. This is a useful strategy to insidiously put the blame on the victim. This blame-the-victim attitude has thankfully long been outdated in mainstream Indian media, as far as direct reference goes, but strategies such as the one mentioned above still persist. These work on a more sub-conscious level and as such are all the more difficult to identify.

The implicating of the victim in the crime is seen not just in the choice of photograph but also in the representation of Jessica as 'brave' in refusing to serve alcohol. The setting of the incident too has been overemphasized. The portrayal of Jessica as the high profile model and bar maid refusing to serve alcohol, though on one level presented as bare fact, on another level shows the tendency of the media to read the crime not qua crime but as being in a consequential relation with what the victim did. Even though this stance is intended to be complementary, yet it seems inclined to romanticize her victimization and implicate her in her own murder. This kind of attitude takes attention away from the criminal and even lessens his agency and thereby his guilt. The portrayal of the victim as an active participant in the exchange, serves the dual purpose of presenting the woman as seemingly being on an equal footing as men and at the same time perpetuating stereotypes of it-is-always-the-victim's-fault.

The average newspaper reader could perhaps not identify directly with the Jessica Lal episode. Surprisingly little was written about Jessica's social background but whatever little was given, presented her as belonging to a fairly affluent background; the upper-middle class. However, the media was successful in making Jessica's story one of the most discussed issues especially months before it died down. Part of the reason for the inquisitive interest in the issue and the media's preoccupation with it lay in its page 3-like quality. The average newspaper reader's fascination with the glamorous party circuit was well played upon by the media in the presentation of the news. So one might look at the interest generated by the media in this murder case as having, at the most fundamental level, an acknowledgement of the reader's appetite for glamour. This initial interest waned in the months following the incident. Later this story of an upper-middle-class, metropolitan victim gained progressively more support as it started becoming clear to the media that this story had the potential of following the classic David and Goliath trope. The support for justice for Jessica, then, at least in the later stage was premised by the media upon her relative merit to gain sympathy. It did not in other words stem from a non-problematic, unequivocal support for the victim of a crime.

This kind of mapping of an incident of violence on the theme of ultimate victory of the underdog is also seen in the case of Priyadarshini Mattoo. Priyadarshini Mattoo was a 25-year-old law student when she was found raped and murdered at her house in New Delhi on January 23, 1996. On October 17, 2006, the Delhi High Court found Santosh Kumar Singh guilty on both counts of rape and murder and on October 30, the same year awarded him capital punishment. Santosh Kumar Singh, the son of a senior IPS officer, had earlier been acquitted by a trial court in 1999. The trajectory of the reporting of the Mattoo case is somewhat comparable to the Jessica Lal case at least as far as the waxing and waning of media interest is considered. But before going on to that, let me first discuss the media's construction of the figure of a victim in Priyadarshini Mattoo. Priyadarshini's presentation in the media appears far less problematic compared to Jessica Lal. Most mainstream English newspapers presented the case in a sensitive way, maintaining an appropriate degree of outrage at the crime. Nevertheless, blind spots remain. The reports repeatedly focused on Priyadarshini's high moral character, her intelligence and even her talent as a singer. The repeated use of adjectives such as 'shocking' and 'heinous' somehow particularized the relative 'crime-value' of the acts of rape and murder in this case. This by implication makes these crimes themselves context-bound in their enormity. It is reflective of the same kind of attitude that looks at the rape of a prostitute as no crime at all.

This is one of the ways in which patriarchal attitudes are silently affirmed by the media.

The handcuffing of a crime with the character or personality of the victim, particularly in the case of rape, raises an important point about the definition of crime. What makes a particular act criminal? What are the bases for labeling an act as an act of crime? Going by the persistent references to what the victim was doing or did in reports about crimes committed against them, one feels as if the two are intrinsically connected. Theoretically, it marks out crime not as a unilateral act of violation of individual liberty and subvertion of social order but as a form of retaliatory social intercourse with an implied involvement of the victim. Though it does not necessarily imply the legitimacy of a particular instance of crime, it does however present a disturbing possibility. It makes one wonder whether a criminal act may be justified in the light of the victim's behavior. This brings the Hobbesian model of Social Contract to mind. Social Contract theory may serve a useful purpose in understanding crimes of self-defense but on a closer look does not hold water in explaining crimes such as rape.

The interest in these cases, as I mentioned earlier, may be seen as being moulded on the idea of the inversion of order. Both the Jessica Lal and Priyadarshini Mattoo cases were picked up by the media since they exemplified people waging lone battles for justice. The victims themselves became abstractions standing for truth and justice and one might even sense an effacement of the gender issue in the attempt of the media to present these as class issues.

One of the most interesting things that happened in the reporting of these two cases by the media was the virtual conflation of the two in popular imagination. Part of the reason for this was the rough correspondence in the judicial trials that followed these two incidents. This conflation was reflected in the reporting of one case mentioning the other one, as well as in campaigns that started to build up around the two in the peripheral media. This conflation itself may be seen as a dehumanizing move of the non-recognition of the victims as separate individuals. This is symptomatic of a larger social condition which makes one see the victim, especially a female victim of a crime, not as an individual in her own right but as a type. This kind of rhetoric generated by the media then turns the whole master-narrative into a status quo-ist discourse. This is not to say however, that all attempts at a less patriarchal approach to representation of women in media are doomed to failure. What I have tried to show through my paper is that there still is a long way to go for Indian media as far as a balance in the representation of women is concerned.

What is big news is so because something else is not. With hundreds of rapes and murders taking place every day, how is it that some particular cases get much more attention than some others; which are buried deep within the insignificant columns of the middle pages. Real women are forgotten as soon as news about them is. Whether in reporting or in its analysis, it is unfair to make value judgment, but the fact that there is imbalance suggests that the gender sensitivity of media leaves much to be desired. The issues taken up by mainstream media are almost invariably concerned with the urban, metropolitan and (upper) middle class. How many of us have heard of Khurshida Banoo, for instance, who was raped in Jammu? In thousands of cases the victims remain just numbers.

Cases of selective activism rather than a more holistic approach, I would like to suggest, has also much to do with an attempt to privilege certain spaces over others. News about the urban centre, particularly Delhi, are taken up and given central importance making Delhi stand in a metonymic relationship with the nation, a move somewhat comparable to the self-reflexive Bollywood gangster films which are invariably set in Bombay. The metonymy on one level marks out a certain identity for the nation and on another constructs one for the city. Reports about protest marches to India Gate are meant to tell us that Delhi is changing and also that India is. Unfortunately these signs are not enough as far as real change is concerned.

The representation of crime against women in Indian media is reflective of the social attitude to women. While it is heartening to see that there is less and less direct patriarchal rhetoric dished out in the reporting on women, it is also obvious that there is a long way to go in achieving a more gender neutral language and attitude.

Reporting, especially the reporting of gender crimes then, cannot be seen as just another story. If we look closely, we can see its various dimensions unfold, revealing that there is more to a story than what meets the eye.

References

"Jessica Lal Murder Case: All 9 Accused acquitted". *The Times of India.* 21, February, 2006.

Hesford, Wendy S. "Reading Rape Stories: Material Rhetoric and the Trauma of Representation". *College English*, Vol. 62, No. 2. Nov. 1999: 192–221 <http://links.jstor.org/sici?sici=00100994%28199911%2962%3A2%3C192%3ARRSMRA %3E2.0.CO%3B2-G>

"Manu gets life term for killing Jessica". *The Times of India.* 20 December 2006. < http://timesofindia.indiatimes.com/articleshow/866102.cms>

"Mattoo Birthday: Memories, March for Justice". *The Times of India.* 23 July 2006: 1.

Tuchman Gaye. "Women's Depiction by the Mass Media" *Signs*, Vol. 4, No. 3 1979: 528–542.

Watkins, S. Craig, Rana, A. Emerson. "Feminist Media Criticism and Feminist Media Practices" *Annals of the American Academy of Political and Social Science*, Vol. 571, *Feminist Views of the Social Sciences.* Sep. 2000: 151–166.